About the Author

Mdude Mpaluka Nyagali is a political activist in Tanzania, focusing on civil rights and good governance.

Five Years of Pain

Mdude Nyagali

Five Years of Pain

Olympia Publishers
London

www.olympiapublishers.com
OLYMPIA PAPERBACK EDITION

Copyright © Mdude Nyagali 2024

The right of Mdude Nyagali to be identified as author of this work has been asserted in accordance with sections 77 and 78 of the Copyright, Designs and Patents Act 1988.

All Rights Reserved

No reproduction, copy or transmission of this publication may be made without written permission.
No paragraph of this publication may be reproduced, copied or transmitted save with the written permission of the publisher, or in accordance with the provisions of the Copyright Act 1956 (as amended).

Any person who commits any unauthorised act in relation to this publication may be liable to criminal prosecution and civil claims for damage.

A CIP catalogue record for this title is available from the British Library.

ISBN: 978-1-80439-490-8

This book is memoir. It reflects the author's present recollections of experiences over time. Some names and characteristics have been changed, some events have been compressed, and some dialogue has been recreated.

First Published in 2024

Olympia Publishers
Tallis House
2 Tallis Street
London
EC4Y 0AB

Printed in Great Britain

Dedication

I am dedicating this book to my three children, who are Derick Nyagali, Denis Nyagali, and Ten_CG Nyagali.

Acknowledgments

In fact, I have a long list of people who played their roles in making this project a success. This book of pains and sufferings is the product of advice I received from my close friends behind me. I sincerely thank all those people whose various contributions led to the completion of this book. I thank some of the lawyers, including Advocate Tundu Lissu, Boniface Mwabukusi, and others for their advice, especially on the chapters related to the laws. I thank the human rights activists Maria Sarungi, Liberatus Mwang'ombe, and others for their inspiration to complete the writing of this book. I also thank my friends, including Basil Lema and others, for being by my side throughout the writing of this book.

GREETINGS

To the torturers and the tortured.
To the activists and the silent.
To those feasting and those mourning.
Kindly, receive my sincere greetings.

INTRODUCTION

I started to collect and keep the stories of the sufferings I was going through during the brutal regime of President Magufuli since 2016. My goal was to keep the memories of these sufferings for myself and other people. Every incident that happened to me, I wrote and kept it without thinking that one day I will collect all the stories of suffering and put them in a book as it is has happened today.

These sufferings have generally made me stronger and made me more and more fierce in fighting for justice and good governance in my nation. These sufferings have increased my courage a hundred times different from what I was before. At the moment, I can, without fear, stand and rebuke any public leader when I see him violating people's rights and good governance.

In the first and second chapters of this book, **Five Years of Pain**, I recount the brutality of the Tanzanian police force and National Security against me, including being arrested against laws of the country, kidnapped, tortured, brutally transported, and detained against the laws of Tanzania.

In the third chapter of this book, I narrated on various incidents, including the one in which The Department of National Security used a woman to establish a romantic relationship between her and me so that it would be easy to catch me. I have also written on how I was saved by one of the employees from that department, who alerted me on evil plots against me as set by the state.

The fourth and fifth chapters are a narration of the false accusations against me. In that case, I was accused of ***drugs trafficking***, a case that caused me to be detained in prison for four hundred and fourteen days as those charges are not bailable by the laws of Tanzania. In those chapters, there is a tale of entire process of this case as it was conducted in court as well as my defense against the Republic.

Chapter Six is a narrative of ***Prison Life***. In this chapter, I have narrated many events that I witnessed by my own eyes. These included prisons hosting prisoners three times than their actual capacity. There is the truth that prisons are mostly populated by detainees than the prisoners due to delay of investigations and trials of their cases. I have also narrated the poor and inhumane diet, accommodation, and medical services as well as the essence of some prisoners and detainees engaging themselves in homosexuality, all in search of a better life in prison.

Chapter Seven and Eight are the narratives of the judgment of the case against me in relation to the charges of drug trafficking, as well as my position in the struggle for justice and good governance in my nation.

Dear friends, I invite you to read this book and join me in the struggle for justice and good governance.

Mdude M. Nyagali.

I
CIVIL TORTURING FORCE

"There are pains and sufferings to take, in a course of fighting for justice, for the benefit of the whole community, and for making you stronger and rational."
– Mdude Nyagali

In that building, there was a special room for torturing people. They named it Guantanamo Bay.

It all began at the end of July 2016 when the Chairman of Tanzania's main opposition party, CHADEMA, Hon. Freeman Mbowe, announced a special anti-dictatorial operation in Tanzania, which was to be named 'Operation UKUTA.' Giving further clarification affront media, Hon. Mbowe said, 'UKUTA is synonymous with Umoja wa Kupambana na Udikteta Tanzania (a unity against dictatorship in Tanzania).' Mbowe asserted that what was then happening in the country as a serious indication that the country was falling into the hands of absolute dictatorship. He called all defenders of peace, justice, and democracy in Tanzania, with a good faith, to engage in Operation UKUTA. On the same note, Hon. Mbowe declared 1 September 2016 a national day of peaceful demonstration against dictatorship in Tanzania.

Following the announcement of peaceful demonstration, some police commanders from different regions responded by issuing statements of threat to people who agreed with Hon. Mbowe and those who were ready to participate in the demonstration. Among them, was the then commander of police in Dar es Salaam Special Zone, Commissioner Simon Sirro, who assured the demonstration would not take place and that the police force was planning to stop it by any means. In the capital city Dodoma, the Regional Police Commander, Senior Assistant Commissioner Lazaro Mambosasa said that the demonstration was illegal and should not be supported by the people of his area, and that already some members of the party – CHADEMA, who are influencing people to take part in the protest, were known and that stern legal action would be taken against them. Thus, according to the leaders of the police force, a peaceful protest demanding justice was a crime and must be vigorously confronted. There were a lot of threat from one region to another. Many CHADEMA leaders and activists were arrested, and many threats were issued to them and their families.

On 28 May 2017, President Magufuli appointed Simon Sirro in the position of country's Inspector General of Police, who then in August, that same year, appointed Dodoma's Lazaro Mambosasa to become the commander of Dar es Salaam special zone. It was an act of promotion to faithful disciples of Magufuli's dictatorial regime.

***

I was one of the few people who campaigned for operation UKUTA and convinced people to join peaceful demonstration. In larger part, I used my social media pages to influence people, ignoring threats from police officers and politician of the ruling party, CCM. I pleaded with the public to come out and support peaceful protests and not to surrender to threats and intimidation posed by police force. I was confident because our intention was not to break peace but to defend democracy, love, and solidarity of our nation. Little did I know is that the threats were not only verbal but also came from hearts of those in power, and there were already plans to use force to brutally stop groups of people and individuals who were inciting protests in any way, anywhere. I didn't know I was one of the most targeted people.

It was summer morning, around eight a.m. on Friday August 26, 2016, five days before the planned demonstration. I was at home sleeping. Suddenly, I heard a loud bang on the front door. I woke up carelessly and went to check the door with only a towel around my waist. I was not anticipating a dangerous moment because I had never experienced such a thing, or perhaps I had not realized the real picture of the fifth-phase government. As soon as I opened the door, it was pushed by people from outside. I helplessly fell onto the floor as four people forcefully entered the house, one of them holding a submachine gun, commonly used by the Tanzanian police force. I was able to recognize faces and names of three of them, except the one who carried the gun. However, his face was not so strange. All of these men were police officers serving at Vwawa Central Police Station in Songwe region. In that raid, they were all in plain clothes. Their names were Nisile Mwaitenda, a corporal; Julius Mkama, a sergeant; and Bashale, a constable. The fourth one I came to know later by the name of Constable Rafael. He is now deceased.

I identified these officers for a number of reasons; I used to see them oftentimes around my workplace, situated between two to three hundred meters from the Vwawa Central Police Station building. From my workplace, I could see policemen marching every morning. Besides that, I also provided services to some of them at my workplace by repairing their cell phones and personal computers. Sergeant Julius, who is now retired, once brought to me his default Tecno cell phone that I repaired. Corporal Nisile, nicknamed 'Nisi,' used to visit my workplace oftentimes. On one occasion, he brought to me his dysfunctional Samsung Galaxy mobile phone, which I fixed. He got the mobile phone from his brother Kennedy Mwaipaja, who lives in the neighboring country Malawi and who was my childhood friend. The closest of these invaders was Constable Bashale, who was my neighbor from the third house. It was very easy for them to find me at home whenever they wanted; as I never knew, they were looking for me.

"What is going on?" I asked, while lying helplessly on the floor. None of them uttered a word. Nisile handcuffed me. Then he pressed me with his knee on my chest so that I cannot trouble him. By then, the other officers had already entered my room. When they came out, I saw them holding my mobile phones and my laptop. That vague arrest and capture of my cell phones made me think that I was going to start that day in cell. But why! How do I go to the police center while naked? I asked them to allow me putting on clothes. Then Rafael entered my room and came out with a pair of trousers and a shirt. He threw them on the couch. With some difficult, since I was handcuffed, I tried to get up and successfully put on trousers, but I couldn't do the same for a shirt. They pulled me naked chest with a shirt hanging on my shoulder, escorted me out.

There were three cars outside my home; black Toyota Harrier, dark bluish Toyota Prado, and a cream Toyota Saloon. I managed to memorize the plate number of the Toyota Saloon which carried me to the Vwawa Central Police Station. They were T726 DGW. I later came to track down from the revenue authority and realized that the vehicle belonged to Sergeant Julius Mkama. My house was searched and some of my property was confiscated without a search warrant or an independent witness, contrary to the laws of our country. They took me to Vwawa Central Police Station in Songwe region. All this were done to me without being told exactly what my crime was.

At the station, I was welcomed by beatings from the receptionists at the front desk of the station together with those who arrested me. I longed to see at least one officer sympathizing on me, but there was none. Their faces reflected the hatred that filled their hearts. Just like a hungry hyena jumps on carcass, so did these beaters brutally beat me. It was as if they were eagerly waiting for the day of my arrest. I believe it was not just hatred, but politically motivated hate, which was fueled by President Magufuli, who always uttered hate speech against his political opponents since from first day he took office.

I was later transferred to the office of Songwe Regional Police Commander, the then Assistant Commissioner of Police Mathias Lucas Nyange. It was my first time to meet this person.

When I was ushered into his office, the regional police commander (RPC) Nyange got up from his chair and approached me. He angrily asked me, "Are you the dog called Mdude who has been abusing President Magufuli on social media?"

I replied that I am not a dog but a human being and I was born to a woman who is also a human being.

He approached me more angrily and told me, "You dare answer me that way? Hear you, dog, the fourth-phase government under President Kikwete was the one that accepted criticisms. You could play with it and even bruise its buttock, but this fifth-phase government under President Magufuli will not be touched on the buttocks by your nonsense criticisms. You must thank your God you were arrested in the morning at the sight of people, but had we arrested you at night without witnesses, we would've killed or thrown you in the wild."

After uttering those words, RPC Nyange ordered the officers to take me out of his office while they awaited for further instructions from the police force headquarters on what should be done to me.

***

They took me out of the RPC's office, and more officers showed up, eager to see me. I heard one say, "Who is this Mdude Nyagali, we want to know?" And another asked, "Is this the prey who dare touching beards of lion?" Another one mocked and spat on my face, while others threw water bottles at me. I was unable to protect myself with my hands because of the handcuffs. As if that wasn't enough, one of the police officers suggested to his colleagues to take me to a room he called "Guantanamo Bay" to "teach me good manners." I knew nothing of Guantanamo Bay in Songwe. All I knew about Guantanamo Bay was that it was a popular island used by US Army to imprison terrorist, and this island is in Cuba. There is news of the brutal treatment of prisoners in the Guantanamo Bay prison, and now, it seemed, Guantamano had its own branch in Songwe, Tanzania!

I was taken into the room, still handcuffed. It was a dirty and darky room was full of some kinds of equipment seemed to be special for torturing people. Now I realized Guantanamo Bay was a special torture chamber inside the Songwe Regional Police Station—a place many Tanzanians believed to be an office responsible for their security and safety of their properties. Most Tanzanians are not aware of these extra activities—torturing people—in police stations, until they become targets. The surroundings of the room signaled as if the construction was underway. Its floor was filled with remnants of baked clay, and its roof was barely covered with wood and iron sheets. There were three wooden chairs, two wooden stools, and a table on which lay a shirt stained with blood.

They made me lay down on my back and tied my legs with a hemp rope. My hands, still handcuffed, were brought them to meet with my leg and tied them together. Now my hands and feet were tied together. There was a rope hanging from a rooftop, which they connected it to my already tied hands and legs, and that made me appear like a chameleon hanging upside down. For that, I felt a very severe back pains, especially at the loin. I produced a sound of excruciating pain and cry out in agony as I asked what wrong have I done to them. Why are you doing this to me? Their response was, "You're crying! Wait and see. We are not done yet. This is just the beginning!"

The pain intensified as they placed a large stone on my chest while I was still hanging, that means my arms and legs were carrying the weight of my body and the stone. Then Constable Rafael grabbed a large stick with a handle and a knot at the end, popularly known as "Fatuma", and used it to strike on my knees, elbows, and soles. Exhausted, he handed the stick to other officers, who continued to beat me in turns while others poured cold water on me. One of them was responsible for photographing and recording videos of my torture, saying that he would publish them on the 'WhatsApp' group of police force – Tanzania as they wanted to see as to whether I'm disciplined enough through the beatings. I do not remember how long the beatings lasted as I began to lose my sight and hearing, and after a while I did not know what was going on. I lost consciousness.

When I regained consciousness, I found myself on the floor with my legs untied and the stone removed from my chest. My hands still handcuffed. The floor was empty, muddy, and my body was worn out, as if I had been picked up from a trash can. My pants were full of mud and because I was bare chested, my body had taken the color of the dirt of that room. They dragged me and threw me into to a cell. Pains were still killing me and no one bothered to give any help.

Contrary to Tanzanian laws, the police even prevented my relatives from coming to see me and bring me food. Even when my lawyer, Isaack Chingilile, arrived, he was not told what I was charged against. Attorney Chingilile came on behalf of my lawyer Boniface Mwabukusi, who was informed of my arrest by a neighbor whom I had asked to call him when I was taken from my home. My complain to be given right to see my relatives and lawyer did not get an ear until when the meeting of police high ranked officers sate and only then they permitted Advocate Chingilile to see me then I first met a person to talk to from my side.

Mr. Chingilile expressed his displeasure with the police force for torturing me in violation of the country's laws. At that time, I was still being tortured and the charges were not made public. He urged the police officers to take me to the hospital for treatment, as continuing to detain me without medical care was illegal and against human rights. But they ignored him.

***

By 27 August 2016, around eight o'clock in the evening while still in custody, I had not received any treatment. My body was in severe pain and my legs had swollen. They took me out of the cell and threw me into police's vehicle. It was Toyota Land Cruiser Pickup, a common type of vehicle used by the Tanzanian police force. They untied my hands and then tied them separately to the bars that made a body of the car. So, I stood up in the car as my two hands tied from either side.

A journey was about to begin, not knowing where I was being taken. Six armed police officers jumped into the car. Among them were those four who arrested me two days earlier. The other two were AIP Luka, who I personally know, and a policewoman who I came to know later as AIP Luka's spouse. In that Journey, AIP Luka seemed to be a leader of the mission ahead. One officer blindfolded me before the start of the journey, but I was able to note the direction of movement. It was moving in the direction of Mbeya region. About an hour later, the car stopped.

There were some movements and voices outside. It seemed like a handover procedure. In the car, with my head bowed and my face blindfolded, I could overhear one officer talking on the phone, saying, "I am at a field force camp at Forest, and we have a trip to Dar es Salaam to transport the suspect, so we will see each other when I return." It was then that I realized I was now in Mbeya, at Forest area where the field force unit camp is, and that I was to be transported to Dar es Salaam. The officers who transported me to the camp in Mbeya untied and dropped me off, and shifted me to another vehicle that looked similar to the previous one. A journey of over 800 miles was waiting me ahead in an open car, with my naked chest exposed to endure and intense cold weather of the southern highlands, and whatever came along the way. Only God Himself knows. Fear welled up in my heart as I was giving in to the intense pain all over the body.

However, I never forgot to say at least a short prayer asking God to stand by my side. He is God of justice.

After completing their handover process, one officer from Mbeya office asked why I was just handcuffed while my legs left untied! One Songwe officer replied, "We hit him so hard he couldn't walk and his legs are swollen so we didn't see the need to tie his legs."

The Mbeya officer was angered and asked, "Do you feel sorry for him? Is this your brother? Let me show you!"

He then collected my legs, tied them up with a rope, and then the journey began. It was a long, arduous journey of more than 800 miles. The road from Mbeya to Iringa was under construction, the vehicles took through more and more slippery paths that were off the shelf and caused it to dance here and there. That made handcuffs to peel off my hands and cause sores. The cold weather was numbing me, especially in a region between Makambako to Mafinga. It was too cold to be able to feel pains in my wound and sores. I tried to ask for the help of at least a shirt to cover me, but my plea only turned to be ridiculous statements. This is like a tale story, but that's how I was brutally transported from Songwe to Dar es Salaam.

Perhaps one could wonder why the officers were so rude and cruel to me. The answer is simple and many people already know. Our brothers in uniform are dressed in political fanaticism and are using government facilities at their hands to contain political opponents of the ruling part CCM. Many of them are deceived and made to believe and see themselves as part of the rulers. They see themselves as defense wing of CCM government instead of an organ to protect citizens and their properties without political biasness. They miss a simple truth that they are civil servants and chosen to be servants of the rulers. Who taught the police officers that CCM's political opponents deserves to be tortured, oppressed, and deprived of their humanity and even their lives? Who taught the police officers that the political opponents of CCM are the enemies of our nation? And this fallacy is being fed to all organs of the state so that CCM will use them to sustain in power.

I remember one time in prison when I met a gentleman named Elkanah Mathias Konga. The man and his three accomplices had been sentenced to six months in prison or pay a fine amounting to TZS 200,000 for alleged negligence and loitering offenses. The sentence was handed down by the Iyunga primary Court. Mr. Konga told me how he and his colleagues were arrested at night and joined together with other people arrested elsewhere in Mbeya city. Then, being arrested and taken to a police car, officers asked if any one among them had a CCM's party membership card so they can release them. According to Mr. Konga, it turned out to be only two of the arrested sixteen had CCM cards, and in fact, the two were released and others were told to pay twenty to fifty thousand shillings to be released. Elkana Konga and others who lacked money were brought to trial for negligence and disorderly conduct. The incident and many others made me continue to believe that our police force is dressed in political fanaticism

***

On the afternoon of 28 August 2016, we arrived at Dar es Salaam and I was detained at Oysterbay police station in the Kinondoni district. God is great; when I was ushered into the cell, I met a young man named Raffi Juma, who was arrested for selling T-shirts with messages that encouraged operation UKUTA. Mr.

Raffi recognized me immediately. He encouraged me while tears were streaming down his cheek. He and other inmates helped to wash my wounds, which were covered by blood clots and mud. They also gave me food and water. That was my first time eating food and drinking water since I was arrested at my home two days before. I really thanked God.

The next day, after arriving in Dar es Salaam, on 29 August 2016, I was taken out of police station and loaded onto a white Land Cruiser Hardtop. Four people in plain clothes were in the car, and I was the fifth. I thought I was being taken to court, but it was not the case. Instead, I was taken to another place for more torture and 'interrogation.' My friend Raffi seemed very nervous and anxious when I was taken from remand. I think he felt that they were taking me to an unsafe place.

While in the car through the window, I saw a man I did not recognize but was in clothes that depicted CHADEMA affiliation, a khaki combat suit. The man boldly approached the car I was in, and then asked the officers guarding me, "Where are you taking Mdude to?" He continued, "I brought him tea after hearing he had been brought here from Songwe. A police officer told me to wait until later, only to see you are taking him out and put him in this car before I meet him." Having said that, one of the officers pushed the man and told him to stay away. The driver then started the car and sped off. I never met that man before, and even now, I do not remember his face.

When the car hit the highway, they blindfolded me so I couldn't see where we were going. I was very scared, but I trusted God to save me from claws of these devils.

As the car continued to move at high speed, one of the officers inside the car asked me, "Have you told your CHADEMA brothers that you are at the Oysterbay station?"

To that I replied, "Police took my phones and laptop and refused to let me in contact with anyone. How can I contact people and let them know I am at Oysterbay station?"

He then tasked me, "Do you know where you are going?" I said I don't know.

"You are going to find out as we arrive," he threatened.

After a while, they uncovered my face and let me look outside the car. I saw that we were entering a house surrounded by a high fence, making it was difficult for anyone outside to know what was going on inside or the other way round.

While still in the car, I saw three women sitting at a veranda of the house. They were in plain clothes, having tea. I heard one of them say, "You have brought Mdude whose CHADEMA supporters are complaining on social media that he has been beaten and his legs broken? Now let him come down and walk." His companions supported that idea and started to yell repeatedly, "Come down and walk! Let him get down and walk!"

Then one of the officers who brought me to the house yelled to me, "Have you not heard! Come down and walk." I cried to that officer, "Brother, I am a fellow human being and a fellow Tanzanian. Please help me. I can't get out of the car and walk without help. You helped me at the station!"

Angrily, the officer pulled me down, and I fell on the ground. I felt excruciating pain. Dissatisfied, he kicked me and told me to get up and walk on my own without anyone's help. I replied, "I can't, brother."

As he raged on, he slapped my back to force me to stand up and jump a little helplessly. It was as if he wanted to show his obedience to the statement of the woman who told me to come down and walk. I was in so much pain. My heart was full of anger, and I swore to revenge for this atrocity I was subjected to.

But at that time, I had no power. Even now, I have left it to God himself. After I failed to walk despite his force and beatings, the officer dragged me into the room inside that house and left me there. The room had a small window through which I could see in the distance the flag of the Democratic Republic of Congo (DRC). The flag was not far because, despite being unable to stand, I could still see it through a tiny window looking out from the floor where I was sitting.

From the other rooms of the house, I heard the voice of someone crying bitterly as he begged for help. Surely, that is the house of the devil. A moment later, the door was opened. I was taken to a living room. There were fresh blood spatters all over the place, a sign that someone had recently bled. Maybe it was the one I heard crying bitterly while I was in the room.

Then I realized I was amidst armed men with various equipment for torture.

One of those people who seemed to be older than others were and as their leader stood still and asked me, "Do you know us?" I answered, "No." He told me, "We are the government, and we want to interview you, but we have our own procedure when interviewing someone." "The first thing you have to do is to take off all your clothes. You will be beaten by these guys naked, and then we will start questioning you about your posts on social media, especially Facebook and Twitter. We will also want you to tell us about your 1 September protest plan."

They stripped me of my clothes and left me naked in that place, in presence of female officers. They ignored the sight of my wounds, trampled on my wounds with great contempt. After being stripped naked, they began to beat me with sticks all over my body. The skin on my swollen feet broke and began to bleed. These people, who lacked humanity, forced me to lick my own blood as well as the fluids that flowed on my feet. I had no choice but to do as they commanded. They photographed me and recorded videos of the torture.

The intense persecution that they called interviews continued. They used pliers to squeeze my testicles so hard. But the worst part was when they were connecting electrical wires with a live stream of electricity with the aim of electrocuting me. Yes, they did that on various parts of my body. I suffered terribly during all the time of torture. Most surprisingly, their interviews aimed at persuading me to switch my membership to the ruling party CCM so that I could remain safe, and then be offered a better job in the government. I asked them for more time to reflect on their wishes, believing that technique would help me out of their hands. They gave me three days to reflect on my move to CCM and threatened me not to report the torture and interviews to anyone. I never had a thought of becoming CCM member.

After the torture session that evening, I was returned to the Oysterbay police station. My consciousness level was so impaired. My whole body was covered with wounds, and tears were flowing all the time because of the intense pain. My body was weak, legs could not stand on their own, my hips ached so badly from the beatings, and even my urine was full bloody. My friend Raffi managed to inform some CHADEMA fellows, who visited him at remand, about me being brought and later released from Oysterbay. He told them about my agonizing health condition.

The news reached many more people who shouted through social media, and finally, on September 1, I was taken to Mwananyamala Hospital. After arriving at the hospital, my wounds were treated, but my left leg seemed to need an X-Ray scan. After leaving the X-Ray room, the brutal police officers insisted on taking me back to the station, although the X-Ray test results were yet to come out. They forcefully returned me to police station against doctor's advice due to my condition. The doctor advised that I be admitted for further treatments, but those officers showed no sign of understanding. The powerless doctor had no choice; he rather prescribed some medication to take at that moment and others for continuation.

On the next day, 2 September, Hon. Tundu Lissu, the then Attorney General of CHADEMA and the Chief whip of the Official Opposition Bloc in the parliament, came to the Oysterbay station and met me there. I informed Hon. Lissu everything from the time I was arrested, a brutal transportation to Dar es Salaam, and tortures I sustained. Hon. Lissu promised to do two things; First, to hold a press conference in which he will inform the public and the world as a whole how the Magufuli regime violates human rights and principles of good governance by using state instruments to torture his political opponents. Second, he promised to file a lawsuit against the police force, asking for me to appear in court or to be granted a bail.

On the evening of 12 September 2016, I was transported from Oysterbay, Dar es Salaam, back to Songwe. I was arraigned in Mbozi district court in Songwe region on the morning of 13 September 2016. Before the court session started, I was fortunate to meet my lawyer Boniface Mwabukusi for the first time since my arrest. He asked if the police had informed me of the reasons for my arrest. I replied to the lawyer that until this time, as brought before the court I had not being informed of my accusations.

According to Tanzanian laws, a suspect must be informed of his or her condemnations before being arrested. I was not notified. But Tanzanian law also requires that a suspect be brought to justice within twenty-four hours of his arrest. But I was detained by the police for seventeen days without trial.

My close friends and relatives were not allowed to enter the courtroom. They were chased away by armed police officers and then themselves filled the room. I was looked at as a bad person in the nation, I felt lonely. But I kept on trusting God.

In the presence of the resident magistrate of the Mbozi district court, the state prosecutor read to me charges of making false statements through social media that could cause incitement in the community against the government of President Magufuli. The case was registered as case number 128 of 2016.

On April 18, 2017, the court ruled in my favor. Reading the verdict Megistrate N.L. Chami said, "The prosecution failed to substantiate the allegations and that this court acquits Mr. Mdude Mpaluka Nyagali."

Despite the happiness gained by me after being acquitted, I remained with many questions as to whether government's commitment was good for me.

***

On November 1, 2017, while in my workplace at Vwawa in Songwe region, I was arrested again by the police officers. One of them who introduced himself to me as Diventin J. Nyahoro with the rank of Inspector informed me that he had been instructed by his superior that I should be arrested and remanded in custody. When I inquired about the charges, he replied that he did not know but he was carrying out an order issued by his supervisor. I was taken to the Vwawa police station and remanded in custody without any known allegation.

On 2 November 2017, I started a hunger strike until my allegations were made public. On 3 November 2017, I was taken to the Songwe's Regional Criminal Investigation Office. Inside the office was the regional criminal officer (RCO) himself along with other senior officers. The RCO wanted me to explain why I did not want to eat or drink. I replied that I needed to first know the charges against me. But instead of informing me of my allegations, he began to threaten me that if his predecessors failed to shrewdly deal with me, he would surely harm me. And that I will never be seen again in the world. After his threats, he ordered me to be remanded in custody.

That same night officers took me out of the remand and loaded me into a Land Cruiser Pickup, tied my hands to the bars in the car, and started to drive away. The car had plate numbers resembling those of neighboring country Zambia. But the occupants of the vehicle were Tanzanian police officers. It was another long journey from Vwawa in Songwe region to Dar es Salaam in almost the same style I was transported in August 2016. We arrived on the next day and on 4 November, I was taken to the central police station at Posta Dar es Salaam and got remanded there. Until then, I had not been notified of the allegations against me.

That night an officer came in to check on all the detainees in custody. The officer, whose name I did not know, seemed to know me well and encouraged me. I took the opportunity to ask him to inform my friend Paschal Haonga, who was then a member of the parliament for Mbozi constituency that I was being held at the station and needed legal aid. He asked me if I remember my friend's phone number and if I do; I should give it to him. Without wasting any time, I gave it to him and he promised to deliver my message to Hon. Paschal Haonga. On November 5, my lawyer arrived at the station and informed me that he had received information through my friend Hon. Paschal Haonga. I was starting to get weaker because I was on hunger strike until my charges were clear. My lawyer urged me to start eating and that he was going to file a lawsuit in the high court to require the police to take me to court for legal proceedings rather than to continue to detain me illegally. After consulting my lawyer, I called off the strike and started eating.

Two days later, I was transferred to another room and placed in solitary confinement. There, I could not meet my relatives or my lawyer. I was not able to meet anybody. The room was dark with a small window at the top. I stayed in that room for ten days without meeting anyone other than the officer who brought me food. Later another person was brought into the room and we became two in the cell. The man was a Rwandan citizen and told me that his crime was to enter cross the Tanzania border without a permit. But I was worried because he was asking me so many questions about the movement and politics in the country.

On November 20, I was transported back to Vwawa in Songwe region. Finally, on November 21, I was taken to court after being detained unlawfully by the police for twenty-one days contrary to Tanzanian and international laws. In all that period of detention, I was not informed of my wrongdoings, neither was my lawyer. The police prosecutor stood before the court and referred to my case as case number 144 of 2017. After that, he started reading the charges against me, that I am accused of publishing false, hateful, and provocative statements against President Magufuli via my Twitter page. It was the first time for me and my lawyer to be informed of the allegations since I was arrested twenty-one days ago. The case was later dismissed by the court after the prosecution failed to bring witnesses to substantiate the allegations.

It became a tradition of Tanzania's Police Force to arrest and detains me and denying me of my legal rights including the right to contact my lawyer and being informed of the charges against me. They even refuse to adhere to the time required by law to bring the arrested to the court of law. Due to these shortcomings, my advocate Boniface Mwabukusi warned me that whenever arrested, I should not accept to be interrogated without his presence all in avoidance of any possible sabotage by the police.

II
MORE TORTURINGS

"The good that we strive for is so much more than all the sufferings we experience."
– Matt. Francis of Assisi

One morning in mid-July 2018, while in my office at Vwawa, Mbozi district in Songwe region, I received a call from one 'John Doe.' This person, I once contacted in March 2018, as will be explained in the next chapter. In a very gentle voice, 'John Doe' warned me that there was a group of national security people who were in the convoy of the Vice President Hon. Samia Suluhu Hassan in her visit to Songwe and Mbeya regions has been given two main responsibilities in here. One was to prove the allegations against Songwe Regional Commissioner Chiku Galawa and then send the results to the President for further actions, and the other was to abduct me. 'John Doe' strongly urged me not to appear in public, he further advised me to leave in secret, without communicating to anyone in any way before those people completes their evil mission against me. I was really confused. I had to hire a motorbike from Vwawa town to the suburb of Shanko to meet Hon. Haonga, a former Mbozi MP. After telling him about the message from someone, I do not know. Hon. Haonga contacted the former Tarime rural MP, Hon. John Heche, who then advised me to flee to Mbeya city through unmonitored paths so that arrangements could be made to transport me to Arusha, where he and Hon. Godbless Lema would make arrangements to evict me abroad. Following the advice of Hon. Heche, Hon. Haonga and I, started the night trek from Shanko to Igamba via Mbozi mission, and then headed to Isansa village, turning right to Nanyala, which is the last village from Songwe to Mbeya. We had to go through those unmonitored paths following advice given to us by Hon. Heche and that unknown person who tipped about the coming of the kidnapers. Although we did not know, whether the person's statement was true or not, our spirits led us to take precautionary measures. Already cases of abductions and disappearances have occurred in the country, so it was important to take precautions when necessary.

We arrived at Mbeya, at midnight, and led our way straight to the residence of Advocate Boniface Mwabukusi without informing him. We went to Advocate Mwabukusi's house for fear of staying in the hotel because the advance team for the Vice President had already begun to arrive in Mbeya and Songwe regions. The kidnappers may have camped somewhere, but it could not be at the home of Advocate Mwabukusi.

At home, we found Mwabukusi and informed him of everything and the purpose of fleeing from my home and that I must travel to Arusha as soon as possible. I stayed there while Hon. Haonga left, I slept at Mwabukusi's residence until the following day, Advocate Mwabukusi and I set off for Arusha from the evening of my second day in Mbeya.

We arrived in Arusha on the following morning. There I met Hon. Lema and Hon. Heche who together had planned my escape trip to Kenya, where they had sought me temporary refuge.

***

On the next day at Arusha while having dinner in the hotel with my hosts and were watching news report on national television TBC. One of the announcements was that the President has revoked the appointment of Songwe Regional Commissioner Chiku Galawa. This statement led me to believe 'John Doe' who warned me about the arrival of a group of security forces sent to investigate the allegations of the Regional Commissioner (RC) and to abduct me. Now, the RC has already been expelled so the task remaining is my abduction.

After the preparations for the departure was completed, Hon. Lema and Heche informed me of the trip, telling me that they had already contacted one of the opposition Kenyan MP who was their friend, and that the MP would receive me and take me to the already prepared residence. Already the vehicle to transport me from Arusha to Kenya has been prepared.

But after deep reflection, my spirit hesitated to continue with the plan of fleeing my country. I told my brothers Heche and Lema that I would not flee my country because of President Magufuli. I will remain back and continue the fight and that I leave my archenemies in the hands of God. These brothers were surprised by the decision because they believed that I would be safe abroad. Hon. Lema urged me to at least stay in Arusha for a while before returning to Songwe, while Heche warned me to be extra careful. Three weeks later, I returned to Songwe by bus. Following all that had happened; I was forced to live with extreme caution. I was changing phone numbers from time to time. I however continued to defend justice whenever I got a chance to do so. Be it on my social media pages, gatherings and even on public transport. I continued to write on social media about justice, equality and democracy in general.

***

Incidents of people being abducted, assaulted, and prosecuted were rampant throughout the first-phase of the fifth term. There are people who are afraid to condemn such acts for fear of being dealt with by the hand of the fifth-phase government, but there are a few who have dared to condemn those deeds, which are against human rights and the principles of good governance. The state media was not ashamed to break the law by dealing with government critics who were not ashamed to denounce acts of human rights violations. I, was not only unashamed to criticize and condemn such acts, but also did not hesitate to name the perpetrators, including President John Magufuli himself. Any right-minded person would not hesitate to associate Magufuli with such acts of human rights violations; draw, torture, abductions, and arraign people. It is because Magufuli has never been heard to denounce such acts, nor has his government ever sought and prosecuted the perpetrators. Furthermore, in some cases—for example in an attempt to kidnap a Tarime based businessman Mr. Zakaria—the kidnappers were found to be national security agents. It is therefore fair enough to say that the people responsible for undertaking search for and arrest the perpetrators of these negligent incidents are the same perpetrators of such incidents.

I did not hesitate to write online and speak publicly—whenever I had the opportunity to condemn such actions. I talked on the streets, at funerals and even at weddings. As a result, the kidnappers did not sleep. They kept on the watch, plotting how to seize me and even cause my disappearance. I know this because I have experience with kidnappers. They kidnapped me,

I knew them, I heard their statements, and I knew their attitudes. They are the people of Magufuli.

***

The kidnappers and their agents kept on threatening me so that I may stop or at least reduce fires of criticism against Magufuli's regime but I did not care. The first to threaten me was their agent Cypran Musiba, a man who had identified himself as an independent activist in defense of President Magufuli. Musiba had no place in the Magufuli government or the ruling CCM. But his statements indicated that he was being used by President Magufuli. Mr. Musiba was so arrogant that he insulted and threatened anyone who opposed President Magufuli. One month before I was abducted, in April 2019, this man held a press conference. At the meeting Musiba was heard saying, "I advise Mdude Chadema to stop insulting the President Magufuli; there is no problem if we finish you for the safety of the remaining fifty-four million citizens of Tanzania." Musiba went on to say that even religious books allow for the 'sacrifice of two persons so that one hundred might be saved.' He went so far as to say that he and his fellow activists will fight anybody whom they believe is insulting President Magufuli on social media.

In the same month, another man known as Abusadik Banzi, appeared and sent me a text message on my Facebook page saying, "Your days are numbered and will soon find you like your friend Tundu Lissu." Of course, this man was referring to the incident of September 7, 2017, when Hon. Tundu Lissu was attacked thirty-eight bullets fired to him, of which sixteen entered his body. The crime, which took place at government leaders' residence in Area D—Dodoma, has not been investigated to-date.

I decided to track down this man who called himself Abusadik Banzi who threatened my life on his Facebook page, I started by posting on my page about him and on the same day a certain woman sent me a private message informing me that she knew the man so well. The woman who was living outside Tanzania identified Abusadik Banzi by the pictures and names he used on his Facebook page. She informed me that he was a thirty-four-year-old man, a native of Tanga region but at the time was living in Arusha. He graduated from military training in 2007, and later joined the military security school (SUK) in Morogoro region. He also served as a security guard at the Geita Gold Mine in the past, and in 2016 became the leader of the CCM security group popularly known as the Green Guard in Elerai ward, Arusha district, Arusha region. I posted information about this man on my social media pages so that people, especially opposition politicians, and activists, would know him and take great care.

I continued to take precautions and at the same time did not hesitate to express my views and criticize all illicit actions of the government of President Magufuli, which every sound-minded person would equally criticize. At the beginning of May 2019, President Magufuli had an eight-day visit to Mbeya region on his way back from Malawi. I used to live in Vwawa, where the Songwe regional headquarters is located, about thirty miles from the Mbeya Cement factory, which was President Magufuli's final destination in Mbeya region's tour.

I followed the President's visit through major media outlets and social networks while responding to some of his unproductive remarks to the nation. I can proudly say that when the President was holding public meetings with the people of Mbeya, I on my side was holding public meetings through my social media pages, especially on Twitter, responding whenever I saw that the President was misleading. I remember my last message before the abduction was that of criticizing President Magufuli when he blamed the people of Mbeya for electing a member of parliament and councilors from the opposition party, CHADEMA and that is why there is no development. The president told the people of Mbeya that the government would not bring them development as they had chosen the opposition. President Magufuli's statement was not new to Tanzanians as he had stated it several times in other areas and repeated it again and again during the 2020 general election campaign.

I condemned those segregated statement but also questioned if electing CCM is a source of development why in many areas where since independence have never been led by any other party than the ruling TANU party and CCM subsequently, there is still overwhelming poverty? I also questioned why the President engages in party politics during governmental visits by reaping opposition politicians who cross to CCM, and why he engages in party politics while banning other parties from engaging in politics? It is like a boxing match in which one boxer is tied, while the other is free to punch his opponent as he pleases.

But the arguments hurt and probably added to the hijackers' desire to kidnap me. I remember, on Saturday 4 May 2019, I was in my office exchanging ideas with Bishop Erasto Makala of the FPCT church. This old man was a friend of mine who never ceased to encourage me from time to time and prayed for me while emphasizing that God is with me and that I should not give up in defending Tanzanians. As we continued our conversation with Bishop Makala, out of my office came two Land Cruiser Hardtop and Nissan Patrol, all in white color. I could clearly see these cars through my office door, which was open all the time whilst in the office. I did not worry because many people were parking their cars in front of my office when they came to get services at my office or at a nearby NMB bank or to get food at a restaurant opposite my office. What shocked me was that after the cars were parked no one came down, and it was difficult to know the number of people inside the cars as its windows were dark shaded popularly known as tinted.

After few minutes, a man got out of one of the cars, he was of medium height, white, and was wearing a black cap; he walked towards my office and asked if he could get a voucher. I replied, "I don't have voucher." He asked where he could get the voucher, and I replied that the vouchers were out of stock. By that time, the sun was setting and people had begun closing their offices and businesses. In our conversation with Bishop Makala, I asked him to help me get a ride in his car at the time of departure. The bishop came out of the office waiting for me to finish the little work that was left while the 'customers' who asked for the voucher was still inside my office. Suddenly, the presence of the mule man inside made my body feel as if there was a danger facing me. When I raised my eyes to look at the person on his way, I saw something like a pistol at his waist from behind. My mind was not convinced that the cars parked in front of my office a short while ago along with the 'customer' who asked for the vouchers were after me. So later, I turned off my laptop and put it in my bag. As I went out and said good-bye to the young gentleman whom I often left in the office because I in most time left the office just a few steps away from the office, three men suddenly stepped out of the Land Cruiser parked in front of my office, one of whom was the 'customer' who had come to ask for a voucher. The other men approached me from where I was standing; they introduced themselves as police officers, and that they have come to arrest me on various charges of sedition against the government through my Twitter page. I asked the men if they really were police officers and said they came from a police station, they looked at each other, and then one of them told me, "Lower your voice." Then I had to raise my voice and speak loudly, asking them to show me their IDs to prove that they were really police officers. They were still staring at each other. I took my phone out of my pocket and told them to wait for me to call the RCO here in Songwe to confirm if there was a case against me. When they saw it, one of them said, "This one is 'bringing flies' here we must control it early." Then they attacked me, beat me, and snatched me of my cell phones and my laptop bag. I started screaming and call for help as I already knew those were the kidnappers. The noise was frightening, but they had masks, they put on their masks to cover their faces so that they would not be identified. The man with the pistol pulled it out, and put it on my head while ordering me to calm down, but I continued to defend myself believing that crowd was the only gear to save me. I hit the pistol and it fell to the ground. Many people gathered but could not help because some of the hijackers got out of the other car and came to help their colleagues. At once one of them was heard saying, "Scatter those flies." Suddenly, gunfire erupted, and people scattered. The only person left in the area was Bishop Erastus Makala who was at all time calling the name Jesus! Jesus! Jesus! Bishop Makala did not run away. Maybe it was because of his age or courage or maybe he was stunned. Among those captors told Bishop Makala aloud, "Old man, flee now; otherwise, I will squeeze the shit out of you." But Bishop Makala did not leave the area and instead continued to proclaim the name Jesus! Jesus! Jesus!

The hijackers managed to handcuff me and then drag me to the Land Cruiser, open the back doors, and threw me in there like a baggage. They hurried away from the scene.

The scene of the abduction was about 100 to 200 meters away from Vwawa Central Police Station. No doubt, the gunshots fired by the hijackers were well heard at the station, but strangely enough, officers from the station arrived at the scene four hours later—according to eyewitnesses.

After they managed to get me in the car and left, I kept screaming and especially when I found out that, the cars were heading to Mbeya. They wanted to blindfold me, but I struggled to keep my face uncovered. Then they started punching me with a fist and a bottle of beer on my head so hard that it shattered and caused me head injuries. One of the kidnappers, who was the most furious bitterly hit me up and kept asking me angrily as to why I was all the time on social media criticizing President Magufuli when the President is struggling to buy planes and build standard gauge railway (SGR) and roads! The abductor hit me hard on the head while we were in the car as the journey continued, that is, he was beating me with tears streaming down his face until his colleagues told him, "Stop it! You will kill him before we bring him to the authorities."

Blood spurted from my nose, ears, and mouth. My eyes were swollen and I could not see properly. My mouth was covered with tape and my face was wrapped in a cloth. The prospect of survival began to fade especially as a result of the memories of the suffering in 2016. I felt that this time, these people have decided to take my life away. All that left to me, was to ask God to receive my soul.

I lost consciousness.

***

When gained a little consciousness, I noticed the car was parked. I heard a voice from outside the car asking the driver to turn on the car's cabin lights. I realized we were at the checkpoint, and the voice was that of a police officer who wanted to conduct an inspection. I overheard one of the hijackers respond that they were 'task force' from headquarters. I tried to scream for help, but I was 'tied' in my mouth so the voice did not come out loud enough to be heard by people outside the car. The kidnappers started beating me again to keep me quiet.

As the trip progressed, one of the hijackers asked his partner where they could leave him as they were on their way. The interviewee replied that they should leave him alone in the office. So, after about an hour's drive, the car was climbing a hill which, in my opinion, was Iwambi from Mbalizi. The journey continued, and later the car crossed two humps, which I think are at Tazara railway crossing at Iyunga in Mbeya. A little later, the car started to shake due to poor road conditions and as soon as the quake subsided, I heard one hijacker say, "This is the zonal office of these idiots," then the car turned to the left. Then I got an image from my experience of the Mbeya city, the area where the vehicle was shook due to corrugated road is Simike, and the 'stupid office' mentioned is the CHADEMA zonal office located in Kadege area. That corner headed to the offices of the Mbeya Regional Police Commander and the Mbeya Regional High Court. Just a minute or two after the car turned from the main road, it stopped. I suddenly heard sound of gate opening to allow the car to enter. It was calm inside; only the sounds of cars were heard from the main road. My feelings and experiences of the city of Mbeya signaled to me that the place is an office for the

Mbeya Regional Police Commander where there are also offices of the RCO.

I heard the hijackers open the doors and then get down and lock me in the car, leaving me there for a while. Later they came and took me out and laid me on my face. I could not see anything or anyone because of the black cloth they tied around my face. One kidnapper told his colleagues, "Since I am staying here let me say goodbye to this idiot, who have questioned us there as if we are in court and filled us with flies." The abductor started beating me, and what I felt was a whip from the hips, from the thighs to the legs. I was in excruciating pain, but I could not cry because my lips were taped. When he got tired of beating me, he left me lying on the ground. Later, I heard one of the hijackers order his companions to get me into a Nissan Patrol and begin the journey. So, I packed up my luggage and went to the boot of the Nissan Patrol. When I got into the car, one of them told his colleagues his mouth was not properly brushed. Then he started attacking me repeatedly with his fists on my mouth and face. I lost consciousness again.

***

I do not know how far or how long it took, but I woke up and found myself locked in a dimly lit room. The atmosphere was warm despite the fact that inside the room there was a rotating fan. There was nothing of value in the room except one stone, the same as the stones used to mark the boundaries of the squares. The floor of the room was red cement.

The shackles were still tied behind my back, and the tape was covering my mouth. The facial tissue was missing. The suit, I was wearing the day I was abducted, was gone; I was left with only underwear and open chest. My eyes were so swollen that I could hardly see.

I was heartbroken that I was being persecuted for my political views and criticism to President Magufuli! But I gave myself hope that God would fight for me. While in the station, I heard the voice of a woman crying out for help from another room of the house. I also heard the screams and the voices of the men who beat the woman, saying you are sabotaging the government; let us show you that this government is not to be played upon. She cried so hard that I couldn't control myself, and tears came to my eyes even though I didn't know her and I had never seen the woman, I wanted to go and help her but I couldn't. Even now, I feel sorry for the woman not getting a help. I do not know but I wish she has recovered as well as I did, and I do not know if she was a government critic like me or a public servant or any other person. I also don't know where she was abducted from, but I do know that she was one of the many victims without their knowledge being known because they were not celebrities. It has been a great challenge for anonymous people to be affected by these tragedies. Most of them are lost without any noise being heard.

After a while, I heard the door to the room I was in opening. A man entered. He was wearing a glove with blood on his hands, and covered his face with a special mask that made his face invisible. I felt the blood on his gloves would be the blood of the woman I heard crying for help in another room a short while ago.

The man began to punch me repeatedly in the face regardless of the swelling and other injuries I had on my face and head. Blood spurted from the mouth, nose, and mouth. I cried bitterly. I would rather die than continue to suffer like that. I never mentioned Jesus and God as often as I did when facing these beatings.

Later, another joined. He was also wearing mask. He was the one who had no mercy and hit me with a lot of anger. There was a time when he pulled out a pistol and aimed it at my head with the intention of shooting me. His colleague told him enough now; they immediately started arguing to the point of fighting by themselves. Suddenly, another man appeared who appeared to be more prominent than they were and ordered him to stop arguing and then approached the one holding the pistol and demanded that he hand over the pistol. After he has handed the pistol, he ordered them both to come out and then locked me up and left me alone in the room. I was in so many pains. Anger filled my heart. Tears were streaming down my face, my hands clasped behind my back. There was a time when I swore that if I were lucky enough to recover and live, I would surely retaliate against President Magufuli's government, but I remembered that revenge was on God, so I left it to God Himself.

On the following day, from the living room, I heard the voices of people talking, as they were moving closer to where I was. Then I heard someone say, "Bring that Mdude."

Two men came into the room, wrapped a towel around my face, and dragged me along, just as a blind man leads a way. They took me to where they wanted to be. They ordered me to sit down. I heard a voice telling me, "I will be asking you questions and you will answer yes or no."

The man questioned me about my biography from the time I was born until I became an adult. He surprised me because he knew my father and mother and the marital crisis they had. He knew the schools I attended from kindergarten, primary school, and even high school. He also knew that I had dropped out of high school. I never knew the real motives of this person to pursue my affairs this much. Sometimes he repeatedly asked me because my mouth was swollen, and I was feeling severe pain in my jaw, and making difficult it to pronounce some words. After the interview, the interrogator ordered that I be taken back to my room. They pulled me back inside the room and pulled the cloth off my face. I could not see them as they were wearing masks like ninjas. It was not long before other persons entered the room, blindfolded me, and dragged me to the place where they had taken me at first. Someone different from the first one came to the area and wanted to see me. Apparently, my name was very popular in the corridors of these people. They sat me down again, and then I heard the voice of someone giving me a 'sermon.' He started by asking, "Mdude, are you enjoying this life?" I answered, "No." He asked again, "Do you remember this sound?" I replied, "I do not remember." He went on, "In 2016, when you were arrested by the police and then transported from Songwe to Dar es Salaam, do you remember those who took you from the Oysterbay police station for interrogation and then took you back to Oysterbay?" I replied that I do not remember the people, but I do remember the incident.

 He continued with the 'treatise,' "Mdude, do you remember 2016 when we were interviewing you, I warned you at that time that the politics of this country have rejected you. I told you and I assured you that in this case you will come out but leave the opposition politics, and that I will look for opportunities. Strangely, you came out to hold a press conference and began to explain the suffering and my men who took you to Oysterbay, said they took you to coaches, as it is, and the things you were being interviewed for and so on. Now I want you to answer me,

Mdude, how did you know the area at that time while you were in Mikocheni?"

He went on saying that he will not defend me as from now. I wanted to tell him you have never and will never be my advocate but those words ended up in my throat. He continued to speak arrogantly, "I was very supportive to the authority, believing in the suffering you would change and I promised to look for opportunities but you don't want to be helped. You are just like a dying ear. Now pray to your God. All the noise out there for you, saying 'Bring Back Mdude' will not help you." The man said that even the ambassadors of any country would not help me; he said they would kill me, and then they would sit with the ambassadors, talk, and end it. He reminded me of reports of journalist, Jamal Khashoggi being assassinated inside the Saudi embassy's offices in Turkey. He informed me that the authority's meeting going on there that I should be killed or that they should continue to hold me for the rest of my life and that no one would know where I was. He concluded by saying that the issue of my release should be forgotten because if they let me go, I would be harmed, as it looks like I would not calm down but will always keep insulting the Magufuli government. When he finished his 'treatise,' I was taken back to the room where I was in before.

That night I was taken from the original room and taken to another. I was not blindfolded, and the tape that covered my lips was removed. In another room, I found two people wearing facemasks, with a subwoofer. They asked me about my religion, and I replied that I was Christian. They told me to say my last prayer, and I did not hesitate to pray the 'Our Father in Heaven' from Matthew 6: 9–13, after which they turned on the radio loudly and sang a religious song called Ekueme from Nigerian artist Prospa Ochumana. They started beating me with new force.

They started by taking off my shorts and I was left naked. One held a large club and the other held a sword. The one holding the club kept hitting me on my legs, especially on my knees, and when he got tired, he handed the club to another. The one with the sword was slapping me from the back. One blow cut my back and caused me to bleed profusely. Undaunted, they laid down their tools and began punching me on the face. They did not rest; one took a small plastic bottle of water, containing water, and began to hit me hard on my penis. They were saying nothing rather than tormenting me while I was crying in pain. The other one connected electrical wire and placed them on my hips and various parts of the body. They 'shot' me for over ten minutes.

I began to see darkness. I could not even move my finger, and I finally lost consciousness.

When I regained consciousness, I did not know where I was. My hands were not handcuffed and I found myself lying on my face. I managed to get up and sit down but realized that I was wrapped in a towel around my face and mouth. When I took off the towel, I realized I was alone and I was in the wild. I burst into tears of joy as I thanked God.

In the distance, I saw car lights and heard a voice. I tried to stand up and walk but failed. I started crawling towards where I was hearing the sounds of cars as well as seeing lights. I managed to draw closer to the road. Luckily, a young motorcyclist known as, 'Bodaboda' saw me on the side of the road and reported to the village chairman—together the village leadership took me to Mbeya Referral Hospital for further treatments.

I was lately told that the place, where I was found was Inyala along TAZAMA pipeline in Mbeya region. The guy who saw me in the bush was known by the name as Erasto Matingo.

III
DREAMS THAT CAME TO PASS

"A rational leader considers his political opponents as an opportunity to correct himself, but a foolish one treats them with bitter and deadly rivalry."
– Mdude Nyagali

'John Doe'
One day in March 2018, I received a call from 'John Doe,'- this is not his real name as it is not safe to expose him. This was before July 2018, when he called me to tell me about a group of security people who were in the Vice President's convoy. These people are assigned to abduct me. I have explained about this in a previous chapter. So that day, 'John Doe' informed me that he had something serious troubling him and that it was necessary for us to meet face to face so that he could share it with me. I wanted him to let me know more about it, why was I had to necessarily meet him when he could solve the problem in so many ways. He told me that it was an issue on saving my life so it was important to meet, and he chose to meet me in the small town of Laela in Rukwa region. He said that in Laela there will be no one to see him, when he handing over the information aiming at saving my life, and he is already in Rukwa region for special official task which he will complete in two months.

I wondered a lot. Could not this person be among the kidnappers who tortured me and took nude photos and videos of me in 2016, in Dar es Salaam! Is it not that he wants to deliver the pictures and videos they took while interviewing me naked? It troubled my mind, as I was not sure about it.

I thought and imagined about this man for he kept calling me by using different numbers each time. I was amazed to see that more than ten numbers he was using to call me through, seemed to be also connected on WhatsApp all the time, and all of them were available on the air. I felt this person was not alone.

I had to share this with my friend, Harajuku Nzunda, so that if it was to go to Laela, then we would be together. We made the journey from Vwawa in Songwe region to Laela, Sumbawanga District, Rukwa region—about 160 miles away. I did not inform "John Doe" on my trip to Laela, as I wanted to be as careful as I could. We arrived in Laela at one o'clock in the afternoon. We looked for a safer location for us. We agreed to sit at an open and crowded area and then call our host. Laela is a small township along Tunduma – Sumbawanga highway. There are many small huts where people gather to enjoy roast goat meat. We stayed in one of the booths. Then, I phoned our host and informed him that I was at Laela in one of the booths.

He was a little surprised that I started the trip without informing him, but he told me he would come to the location in just half an hour. While we waited for him to arrive, we arranged for Harajuku to stay outside of the hut for precaution and watch us from the distance in case anything happens.

"John Doe" came in as he promised. He did not have to call me in identifying, as he seemed to know me well. He greeted me and introduced himself with the same names he had introduced himself when we communicated on the phone. Without wasting any time, he told me that he was an employee in the Department of National Security and that inside the agency there was a conspiracy to abduct me, but he doesn't support it, and so he sought it necessary to deliver this information to me with an intention to help me start living with maximum precautions as prevention is better than cure.

He told me that there was a special force formed to protect the President's interests against the various people who attacked and criticized him. The force has been tasked with combating opponents of the President and his government. This included journalists who cover bad news against the President and his government as well as all activists who use social media to criticize President Magufuli, myself being among them. The man went on to tell me that there have been many complaints from people close to President Magufuli, that I use harsh language and unhealthy words in my criticism against President Magufuli via my Twitter page and that despite being severely tortured in 2016, but I have not yet corrected myself. Therefore, the only remedy is just to finish me.

My whole body trembled and sweat stripped all over. I stood up and calm myself down in few seconds after hearing those words. I remembered sufferings and torturers, I incurred in 2016, from the so-called taskforce! I was so perplexed to the point of thinking as to whether I should give up politics. However, I questioned myself, how many people who does not do politics and ere already killed. Who am I to run away from death? I encouraged myself and oathed to continue with struggle, as I always believed in God on defending justice and righteousness, I asked the man if he had any thoughts of helping me to avoid them.

He then advised me to take two or three precautionary measures. That I should not eat and drink in bars, and any luxurious places, and instead eat food prepared in my own home by myself, or any trusted family member I live with. He told me it was best to buy drinks, drink at my house, and when I go to shop for groceries and beverages; I must go in an environment where I will not be easily recognized by the people in there. The man told me that this method would help reduce the likelihood of being poisoned.

He warned me about strange women, especially beautiful and attractive women. That, many can be sent and some of them can pretend to be activists like me to see them as my colleagues, and they can even bribe me a lot of money but it is a trap. Through his experience, many people fall into this trap and unknowingly fall into trouble.

He continued to warn me not to walk alone along the road or any other place and instead when I was walking or traveling, I should make sure that I am accompanied by people around me. He also advised me to use public transport like a bus or train as it is very hard to be kidnapped while seen by other people. Finally, he encouraged me and told me not backslide. He concluded that if President Magufuli wins support of all the people, will he stop making mistakes? It is impossible.

After that brief session with Mr. 'John Doe' we said goodbye to each other and I returned home to Songwe on the same day, thinking a lot about taking the precautions as was advised by others. I had every reason to believe the message from 'John Doe.' I believed him. He was one of the agents of life in the midst of a group of deadly agents.

***

On 6 January 2019, I was conducting a working session of the CHADEMA 'membership registration operation' in Mawenzusi village, Mollo ward, Sumbawanga district. I being CHADEMA Training Officer for Nyasa zone was present at the session as a trainer in the operation. In the middle of the session, I got a call from *+96871944262*. I learned later that the numbers indicated that the phone was from Oman. I was forced to give a little break to my fellows and walked out of the session to answer the call. A woman's voice from the other side greeted me harmoniously. She introduced herself by the name of Doka Ole and that she lives in Istanbul, Turkey. Her tribe is a Maasai from Longido but a native of Dodoma, and that her mother is from Tabora. I continued to listen eagerly to find out what the purpose of the call was. She said she was given my number by a friend named Amina who studied with her in Dodoma and is a member of Chadema. Doka Ole told me she had studied with Amina at Jubilee School and one of their teachers was a famous comedian by the name of MC Pilipili. Doka claimed that she had called me to express her feelings, that she had deep feeling of love for me and that she was willing to do anything to help me. She said she had been searching for me for a long time without success, she had sent me many messages on my social media pages, but none have been responded upon. She then had to search for my numbers so that she could contact me directly.

As she continued to express herself, I interrupted her and informed her that my phone was running out of charge and I was in the village, running a party session. Therefore, she should look for me a little bit later. It is true that the phone was running out of charge. So, we said goodbye to each other and hung up the phone. I then returned to continue with the session.

Having returned to Sumbawanga town that evening, I charged the phone and turned on the internet, I found in the WhatsApp message room pictures of a woman taken in various romantic styles. I identified the number of the person who sent the messages as the lady that called whilst in the session. Certainly, this woman was very cute; she had a unique personality, and so charm. It was as if I have struck a million-dollar lottery, but my mind came back. Suddenly the woman called on video via WhatsApp, I received and saw her real face. It's the same one I saw on the pictures she posted on my WhatsApp account. The beauty of her and morphology were the same.

What she needed from me in particular, in her own words is my passion. Sometimes, she even dared make 'video call' while naked and lying romantically on her beautiful bed. She had such a sweet voice that when she called my name 'Mdude,' the whole body shook with excitement. I decided to put myself in a position to do nothing. I did not reject or accept her, but I wanted to spy on her so that I will know what was behind the scenes. She continued with her mission of making daily calls—she called from the morning to evening, explaining how she was dying for my love. She once told me that she was ready to die for me. She reached out and started sending money to me. For example, in February 2019, while I was in Sumbawanga, the Police confiscated my phones after I got into a dispute with them. When I went to the station to bail CHADEMA members who were arrested a day before. The police turned against me and I had to bail myself by leaving my phone with them, and only took my sim lines. I bought a small phone that did not support the Internet, and therefore, did not appear on 'WhatsApp' or other networks. Doka phoned me and asked me where I was, and I gave her the whole story. She asked me if she could send me some money through Western Union, and I replied that I had never used that method before. She said, wait a minute. After about an hour, I received a text message saying that I had been sent TSH 950,000 from the Tanzanian number. Later Doka informed me that she had told her friend in Tanzanian to send me money to buy a phone urgently. She then told me that she will come to Tanzania during her May 2019 vacation, and that she will bring me an iPhone worth $1000 and an Apple laptop worth $3000. I was very thankful to her.

Still memories of caution from 'John Doe' stuck in my mind. The anxiety I had over my life was enough to prevent any feelings of love from someone of the Doka Ole's type. Though my heart acknowledged that she was pretty, yet my mind never accepted with her wishes. I kept asking myself questions; how could this woman, with such beauty lack a man in Turkey, or even Dar es Salaam, till she come to love me from here in the wilderness of Sumbawanga! There was a time, when I could not hide my concern and so I accused her of being sent to arrest me by the kidnappers.

I informed some of my important friends about the news of this woman, especially those who knew the environment I was living in at the time. My friends helped me to search the woman and to identify few things. We first found out that the woman was not in Istanbul as she had told me but was living in Oman. It was after checking where her phone was making contact from. Secondly, we found out that she was not an employee of the immigration department in Turkey as she told me. Three of us found out that the name she had introduced herself to me was not her real name, and she had a page on Facebook that had a different name. But also, in her statements she was very confusing, especially about her citizenship. There was a time when she told me she left Tanzania with her aunt living in Canada, immediately after graduating from high school, and stayed there for a long time, until she was granted Canadian citizenship. I remember she once told me, she works with the immigration department in Turkey, and I asked her how come that a citizen of another country be granted work in an immigration department of another country? She said that she had have been granted Turkish citizenship and was employed by the department because of her multilingual capacity as she was able to speak all languages found in Asia and Europe.

Remembering the warnings given to me by Mr. John Doe, I doubted this woman and kept contacting her with great caution. She went on to insist that on her holiday in May 2019, she must come to Tanzania and stay with me.

At around four in the evening of 4 May 2019, this beautiful woman from Turkey telephoned me via WhatsApp. I received and told her the environment here was not favorite and pleaded with her to call later. That was the day I had a visit from Bishop Erasto Makala in my office at Vwawa. But before she hung up the phone, she asked me where I was, to which I replied that I was in my office. She asked me not to forget to call her later because she has missed me so much, I hung up. About two hours later, a man with a cape came in and asked for a voucher. This is the man I said in the previous chapter that abducted me. I think I made grave mistake to have informed that woman of my current location.

After being abducted and all what happened to me that woman had never called or texted.

***

On 17 December 2018, I received a call from a man who introduced himself as Furaha Kabuje, who is the Pastor of

Pentecostal churches. At the time, he was calling me from Iringa while in his pastoral duties. I had never met Pastor Kabuje before. He told me that he procured my number from the Iringa MP Hon. Peter Msigwa who is also a pastor. He said the main reason, he was looking for me was about a dream he got four days ago, a dream that forced him to get up at night and pray.

Pastor Kabuje told me that in his dream he found himself at a bus stop waiting for public transport to return to his home. Unfortunately, that day there was a serious transportation problem and so he did not get transportation in the area for the long wait. He went on saying that while waiting patiently, he saw Bajaj transport coming but it was so crowded and one of the passengers in it was me, Mdude Nyagali. The pastor said, there was an argument between me and the driver of the Bajaj, and I wanted him to stop to pick up the pastor who was also waiting for transport but the driver refused and defended himself that his Bajaj was full. After further argument, the driver agreed to stop and then carried Pastor Kabuje. The pastor thanked me profusely while the journey continued. The pastor claimed that we arrived at the place and I told him I had reached my destination, so I would get off, and he told me he was not living far from my house so he would come down to pray for me at my house before he gets to his home. In the dream, the pastor said that we went to my house together, and when we arrived, I knelt down and he prayed for me and after that we went out venturing all along to his house. The pastor continued that, as we walked, he heard a voice telling him, "Get Mdude out from there he is in danger." But before he could do anything, a car filled with armed people arrived and he suddenly waked up.

Pastor Kabuje explained to me how the dream made him uncomfortable and even forced him to fast and pray for two days to get the interpretation of the dream. In his words, the Pastor told me that in the dream he was shown that Mdude will get into serious troubles but will not die because there is something God has put in him for the nation of Tanzania. After receiving these answers, Pastor Kabuje phoned me to let me know and advised me to be closer to God because he saw that my work of advocating justice was going to cause me a lot of problems. The incident took place five months before the May 2019 abduction.

IV
TRIAL

"At his best, man is the noblest of all animals; separated from law and justice he is the worst."
– Aristotle

Republic *versus* Mdude Nyagali
On the morning, 13 May 2020, I was arraigned before the Mbeya Resident Magistrate's Court in the city. No relatives, friends, or acquaintances had any information of me being brought before the court. I actually felt like a stranger and lonely because during all three days, I was detained, the police officers denied me the right to report to my relatives.

My case was charged on economic sabotage as suspected of being found with drugs. It was case number 2 of 2020. After reading the indictment, the court did not allow me to say anything because, according to Tanzanian law, economic sabotage offenses are heard and decided only by the High Court. Therefore, this action to be brought before the Resident Magistrate's Court was aimed at following the legal procedure, or in legal language—committal proceeding. This process included matters, such as completing investigations, demonstrations, preparing witnesses and so on. Before being brought before the High Court, which has the legal jurisdiction to hear and decide these cases. Therefore, the case was adjourned until 27 May 2020, and I, the suspect, was taken to the Ruanda prison in Mbeya region.

On 21 May, one week after my incarceration, and one week before his return to court, Counsel Reginald Martin, a lawyer from THRDC, arrived. Two years ago, Attorney Reginald helped me prepare and open civil case against Inspector General of police, IGP Simon Sirro. Of course, he came again to give me legal aid, under the auspices of the Tanzania Human Rights Defenders Coalition (THRDC).

It was then that I discovered that reports of Mdude Nyagali's arrest had spread across the country through the media, especially social media. However, the Mbeya regional police commander spoke in front of the media and informed the public of my arrest and detention. Advocate Reginald therefore obtained the information, and through the THRDC he was instructed to come and represent me in the case. Attorney Reginald told me he would work with lawyers Faraji Mangula and Peter Kibatala who would lead the panel. He told me that there were many other lawyers—about six or seven who had asked to help defend me in court. It was a blessing to me; it encouraged me and gave me a signal that the spirit of the struggle against oppression is still alive.

It is well known that the early period of 2020 was a difficult period for the whole world due to the COVID-19 pandemic, a situation that led to many activities being carried out digitally. As elsewhere, Tanzanian courts have handled some of their cases online. But that was not the case to me as on 27 May 2020, in the morning, the State Attorney, Mr. Namkambe came to the prison to tell the prison officers that my case would not be conducted online like other cases and so they should hurry to take me to court. It so happened.

On that day, the court was strongly guarded and many media outlets were present. Many CHADEMA leaders and members who came to follow the case were barred from entering the courtroom except for a few people. My lawyers and I, Reginald and Faraji were worried, we wondered what was going on. Why the court so strongly guarded and the media outlets is brought in such big number? Or is it that they want to convey a clear message to Magufuli that notorious Mdude has been arrested and charged with economic sabotage? Or is it a continuation of intimidation? Personally, I did not have a quick answer.

The case was mentioned. Then the Attorney for the Republic, Mr. Namkambe asked to remove my case from the court. Then the case on economic sabotage was dropped and the judge said I am free, as the case has been dropped. Only until later, I came to know what was going. As I was leaving the courtroom believing I was free, the clerk of the court mentioned case number 136 of 2020. Immediately a group of police officers attacked me and took me back to the dock. I was really angry and wanted to punch him but my lawyers begged me to stay calm. Then, I was arrested and charged with drug trafficking. However, when the state attorney came to the prison and told the officers to take me to court because my case would not be conducted online, he knew about the game. Even the crowd of police officers deployed in the court ground was there to complete the task of arresting Mdude Nyagali after the release by the court. The charges changed from economic sabotage to drug trafficking. The amount of drug described by the prosecution was 23.4 grams.

The accusation was read to me and I was asked to state if it was true or not, and I replied that it was not true. The court ruled that the defendant's code of innocence, until proven otherwise, would apply. The statement reminded me of the inconveniences I experienced before I was taken to court. I thought to myself, if I am an innocent defendant until proven otherwise, why am I living in prison? It is not right!

***

After being charged with drug trafficking and denied the charges. The state attorney said the investigation was not complete but when the case is called again, we will be ready for a preliminary hearing.

My lawyers wanted me to be granted bail in accordance with Article 13 (6) of the Constitution of Tanzania, which states *'it is forbidden for any person who has been charged with a criminal offense to be treated as a criminal until proven guilty.'* By that logic, bail is the defendant's right and not the prerogative. State attorneys on their side referred to 2017 amendments on Drug Control Act section 29, which removed the word 200g and replaced it with 20g. Twenty in that passage means twenty grams. According to this article, if a defendant is found in possession of drugs weighing more than 20 grams, he or she may not be granted bail. I was accused of being found in possession of drugs weighing 23.4 grams, so according to that clause I could not be granted bail by this court. It seems that the police officers who plotted this case knew about the law that is why, they have made sure that, this sample should necessarily be more than twenty grams so that I would not be granted bail.

But the learned Advocate Reginald Martin insisted that despite the information provided by the prosecution, the defense believes that the court has been empowered to grant bail

Advocate Martin's position is supported by recent decisions in case number 29 of 2019 filed by Dickson Paul Sanga against the Attorney General. The case was heard and decided by the High Court, the Chief Registrar of Dar es Salaam under Judge Masoud and two colleagues, Judge Masabo and Judge Kulita. Attorney Martin promised to bring a decision in the case as early as possible in which the High Court ruled out the clause is unconstitutional provisions that deprive defendants of the right to bail.

My lawyer concluded by stating that the court had the power to grant bail to the accused, "We ask your esteemed court to grant our client bail. That's all."

It was the turn of the state attorney, he said, "I have listened very carefully and with a lot of caution to the statement of the learned defense counsel who has unfortunately failed to present in this court here the reference to the decision he made in defending his argument. I, however, know about the decision he is referring to. What was said in the decision is this: that the government should amend the clause within eighteen months. Since, eighteen months have passed and the government has not made any amendments, then this feature remains the law."

The state attorney continued, "It is a fact that according to Article 13 of the constitution the accused is entitled to bail. But we continue with our position that in this case the defendant does not deserve bail."

After that verbal exchange, Magistrate Z.D. Laizer stated, "I have considered the details of the parties and read the verdict given in the Dickson Paulo Sanga case which the defense counsel referred to here. I have noted that the decisions referred to herein apply to section 148 (5) of the Criminal Procedure Code. I will begin with the information provided by the state attorney Mr.

Namkambe who opposing the accused to be granted bail. Defendant is charged in accordance with the Drug Control Act. Regarding bail, the state attorney has referred to section 29 of the Drug Control Act No. 5 of 2017. This section of the Act deals with offenses that do not allow bail. The two clauses read together violates the defendant's right to bail if he is accused of smuggling drugs from twenty grams or more. The defendant in this case is accused of transporting the drug up to 23.4 grams, meaning that according to the clause referred to, the accused is not eligible for bail."

The magistrate continued, "In counsel no. 29 of 2019 Dickson Paulo Sanga v and Articles 13 (3) and 15 (1), (2) (a) of the Constitution. With regard to the bail, application of the defendant has brought by the defense counsel, the court finds that the submission is not enforceable as the law as it stands is defending itself. On page 43 of the decision, the court stated that, "… and the remainder of section 148 (5) of the Criminal Procedure Code (CPA) which deals with all cases except armed robbery shall remain the same for eighteen months from the date of this judgment."

She continued by saying, "The clause quoted above means that, with the exception of armed robbery offenses, the rest will not be liable until the eighteen-month period stipulated by the government expires. Therefore, the application of the decision may not be implemented until the court-ordered eighteen-month term expires. It will therefore not be possible to use the reference to grant bail to the defendant although I firmly believe that bail is a constitutional right of the defendant and not a privilege."

"These arguments lead this court to the view that the defendant's right to bail is restricted in this law which I have quoted. Therefore, the defense counsel's request for bail is rejected." the magistrate concluded.

Following the court's decision to dismiss my bail application, Advocate Faraji Mangula filed an appeal against the decision so that a formal interpretation could be given by the High Court. At the same time, Advocate Faraji requested a copy of the decision and proceedings of the case.

The court's decision was that the proceedings and the decision on this case would be obtained after the trial, and that the case would be re-assigned to 3 June 2020 for a preliminary hearing, and that I, the defendant, will remain remanded in custody at Ruanda Prison as the bail had been withheld.

***

On 3 June 2020, I was brought back to court, but the case was not heard because my lawyers could not come as they were attending another case in the High Court. It is a legal procedure that when a lawyer has two cases, in courts with different jurisdiction, and if those cases are mentioned or heard at the same time, then the lawyer will have to go to a court hearing in a higher jurisdiction. Therefore, my lawyers went to the High Court. The case was adjourned until 2 July 2020.

On 2 July, the case was conducted online while I was incarcerated. However, the case was adjourned again until 16 July 2020 after the defense counsel Mr. Martin stated that the appeal to the High Court against the judge's decision to deny me bail had not yet been set. "It is true that we have appealed to the high court, but we have not been given a date for our application to be heard," said attorney Martin.

On 16 July 2020, I was brought back to court in person unlike the previous mention when it was conducted digitally. However, my lawyer Mr. Martin, participated through online. On that day, the magistrate was Hon. D Luwungo and the state attorney was Mr. Kihaka.

Advocate Kihaka said the case had come up for mention. "We are currently awaiting the submission of a summons on the appeal by defense counsel in the High Court. We therefore request your court to set another date for the mention of this case."

My case was repeatedly postponed for various reasons. For example, since my lawyers appealed against the decision of the Resident Magistrate's Court to deny me bail, the case was adjourned twelve times because; firstly, awaiting the High Court's decision on my appeal against the deprivation of bail, and secondly, because of the prosecution's failure to complete the investigation on time. And due to the court order that the case should be mentioned within fourteen days for a detainee, my case was at most of time facing adjournment. The case was often conducted online. It was like a tradition that, if the case was run digitally then it was obvious that the case would be adjourned. Magistrates and other court officials did not want the inconvenience to appear in court for the purpose of adjourning the case; they considered it best to do so online. While in prison, the inmates used the office of the assistant prison warden to proceed with their trials online, which however was not effective enough due to poor technology used. Therefore, in cases that required a lengthy hearing, if there was evidence to be presented or a verdict handed down, the accused had to be present in a formal court because of unreliable internet service.

***

The High Court continued to hear my appeal against the denial of bail in writing and finally the judgment of that appeal was scheduled for September 10, 2020. But before the day of judgment, the Court of Appeal in Tanzania quashed the judgment of Judge Masoud and his associates, which would have helped in the appeal against the deprivation of my bail. The reversal of the sentence allowed all offenses to be granted bail, which my lawyers used as a reference to build arguments against my being denied bail. Ironically, the verdict was overturned after the Director of Public Prosecutions (DPP), Biswalo Mganga, filed an appeal with the Tanzanian Court of Appeal against the verdict of Judge Masoud and his associates. So now, the pillar we relied on in our appeal to the High Court collapsed before the September 10 hearing, because our support, Judge Masoud's verdict, did no longer exist. I did not know whether the decision to overturn Judge Masoud and his associate's decision related to the conduct of my case or not! On 10 September, as expected, my appeal against the deprivation of bail was dismissed by the High Court. So the prospect of obtaining bail was dashed and from then on, I accepted the status of continuing to be in detention while the main trial in the Resident Magistrate's Court continued. Still, my case continued to be mentioned and postponed from time to time due to incomplete investigations. It became a habit to go to the office of the assistant prison warden to witness the case being postponed online. And my lawyers knew that the case would be adjourned, so they did not bother to burn fuel from Dar es Salaam to Mbeya, more than 800 miles away. By 29 September 2020, I personally filed a lawsuit. That day I told the court that the appeal against the bail had been dismissed by the High Court, so I ask that the primary case continue. I insisted that, since my lawyers were away, but I would contact them to let them know the date on which the preliminary hearing would begin. The magistrate adjourned the case until 6 October 2020, for the preliminary hearing and I, the accused, will remain in custody. However, when the date came, the case was adjourned until 3 November, when a preliminary hearing was held. That day I was reminded of the charges against me, and I immediately denied the charges.

Then the state attorney read the preliminary information to me. One, that the personal information of the accused and the details of the charges against me are as shown in the indictment; where, my name is Mdude Mpaluka Nyagali, thirty-two years old, Mmwera by tribe, and Christian. Second, that the incident occurred on 11 May 2020 in Mwasote Street, Itezi ward within Mbeya District, Mbeya Region. Third, that on 10 May 2020, the accused was arrested by the Assistant Superintendent of Police (ASP) Sylvester Siame for publishing reports of harassment, fabrications, and insults on social media, and I was taken to the Mbeya Central Police Station for questioning. Fourth, on the next day i.e. 11 May 2020, Assistant Superintendent of Police (ASP) Siame along with other police officers, I the accused, and my lawyer Mr. Fadhili Shombe went to my house, located at Mwasote Street, to do a search. Fifth, that a search was conducted in front of me, the accused, my lawyer, and a member of the ten houses of the area as well as several other officers of the police force. Sixth, that during the search, they found five packages containing substances suspected to be drugs. The items were taken and tested in the laboratory of the Chief Government Chemist of the Mbeya region. Seven, that what was found by the police were 23.4 grams of heroin. The state attorney ended there

Based on that preliminary statement from the state attorney, the court identified the controversial and un-disputing matters; that there is no dispute on my personal information, in the sense of name, age, religion, and place of residence was correct. There was also no dispute about the arrest by police officers on the day and time specified, and a search was conducted at my home on 11 May 2020. Engaging in drug trafficking. The next step is for me and my lawyer Mr. Faraji, prosecutors, and the magistrate to sign on matters not disputed against the ones disputed.

After that action, the state attorney Mr. Saraji told the court that the prosecution is ready to bring witnesses before the court to prove the allegations against me, and my lawyer Mr. Faraji Mangula replied that we are also ready. And the magistrate set a date for the official start of the trial; he mentioned three consecutive days dated 1, 2 and 3 December 2020.

***

Finally, on 1 December 2020, the primary case began to be heard by the prosecution to bring its witnesses. The first prosecution witness was Mr. Jansen Bilaro, a thirty-four-year-old resident of Iwambi, a Christian, and a chemist in a government laboratory. He was sworn in and began giving evidence as led by a state attorney; "I have received a summons to appear in court here while studying in Morogoro," The Witness started and continued, "I am continuing my studies at Sokoine University (SUA) with a master's degree in toxicology science. I have a bachelor's degree in environmental science and management. After being hired, I have attended various trainings locally and abroad. The training is about investigating samples and evidence, as well as the use of different materials used in laboratory tests. After my appointment, I was assigned to work at Ocean Road – Dar es Salaam from 2012."

He went on, "I was transferred to a government chemistry laboratory in Mbeya from 2014."

The state attorney asked him to explain the procedure for conducting a laboratory examination. The witness replied, "Procedurally, when we receive a suspected drug from the police department, it should be accompanied by a letter of inquiry. The recipient of the specimen is a shift chemist. The chemist on duty inspects the object to see if it is related to the details of the attached documents. After inspecting them, he receives them and enters their information in the register and is given a laboratory number. The chemist then marks the specimen and its documents and takes them into the laboratory for examination as the client requested."

The witness continued, "Tests are done twice. There is a preliminary investigation and a satisfactory investigation. Preliminary research involves the appearance of a figure; for example, we look at color and structure, like flour or leaves. It also involves conducting research to find the exact color. A small amount of flour is mixed with a certain chemical to see how the color changes from its origin to another color. This gives us an indication that the powder is a drug."

The State Attorney asked the witness if he remembers on May 12, 2020, where he was and what happened. The witness went on to explain, "On 12 May 2020, I was doing my usual job in the offices of the Chief Chemist of the government of the Southern Highlands Zone. I was the chemist on duty that day. I received a police officer from the Mbeya Regional Investigator's Office. The officer, as I recall, was the Assistant Superintendent of Police, Clement Siame. They came with a letter, a form, and a sample in a nylon bag. The letter was sealed and stamped by the police. In the letter, they asked an official in a state laboratory to conduct an examination on the samples to see if they were indeed drugs."

"I registered the document and gave it laboratory number 132/2020. After registering it, I took the relevant letter, form, and illustration and went to the laboratory for examination. I signed the letter attached to the label to show that I had received it. My goal was that I would be able to recognize the letter anywhere as it would bear my signature."

The State Attorney asked the witness if he could remember the documents he mentioned, and he said he could.

The witness was given a document and identified it as the form used to bring the sample to a government laboratory. The magistrate asked my lawyer if he had any objections, and the lawyer replied that he had no objection. Then form no. DCEA 001, signed on 12 May 2020, was received and admitted as exhibit P1.

The Witness went on to say, "The document contains my signature, which I putted it on 12 May 2020 after receiving the relevant documentation. I request this court to accept this letter as an exhibit P1."

The witness read exhibit P1 and proceeded to inform the court that, "In this case, the client wanted an investigation into the samples submitted to the chemist's office to determine the weight of the samples, including the type of drug and its effects on its user." The witness said the samples were brought to him by the Assistant Superintendent of Police Mr. Siame. I do agree with the fact that the chemist who received the form and the bag containing the samples was himself.

The witness continued, "After receiving the bag containing the samples, I went to the laboratory for testing. I opened the bag and found inside there were five small packets marked A1 to A5. I opened one bag after another. All five bags contained flour and I weighed one by one."

"The client wanted me to check what kind of drug the powder was. I tested sample A1 by taking small amounts and mixing them with Nitric Acid chemicals. The powder changed from white to green, resembling a banana leaf. These changes in color indicate the presence of a chemical called Hydrochloride. I did the same with the samples available in pockets number A2, A3, A4, and A5, and they all gave similar results. This is to say that all five samples changed from white to green, indicating that all of the samples were 'Heroine Hydrochloride' drugs." The witness said that was a preliminary investigation.

The witness continued, "I finally did a satisfactory investigation into the initial results I got. I took a small amount of the sample and mixed it with one of the chemical compounds called Organic Salts so that I could determine the amount of chemicals contained in those samples. This method is technically called Solvent Extraction. I took a sample and tested it on a special measuring device called 'Gas Chromatology.' This experiment convinced me that the sample I tested contained the Heroine Hydrochlorine compound, which is a dangerous drug. I finally published an official statement explaining my findings and details about the side effects of the drug.

These drugs affect human brain. It also makes the user want to use them again and again. This addiction is very dangerous for the user. After completing my investigation, I sealed the remaining sample bags and sealed them with a state chemist stamp and put my signature."

The witness said that after completing the investigation exercise, he wrote an official statement of the results of his investigation and handed it over to his supervisor. He went on to say, "My statement was accompanied by a form and a letter from our client and the procedure I went through in carrying out the investigative exercise. My supervisor is Gasper Mushi, who is a Senior Chemist. The goal was to confirm my work and sign the statement. After receiving the information from me, he inspected it and approved it, signed it, and finally stamped the state chemist's seal. I finally handed over the information to ASP Clement Siame."

When asked how he could identify the report, the witness replied that he would recognize the statement he had prepared as it had his signature, the name of his supervisor, and the seal of the state chemist's laboratory as well as the mark of the Tanzanian government. The witness was given documents. And he realized that this was the information he had prepared based on his analysis. Finally, he asked the court to accept the documents as his evidence in the ongoing case.

My lawyer, Mr. Faraji Mangula, objected to the receipt of the documents as the witness told the court that his statement was accompanied by a letter from the client requesting an investigation. However, the statement he is filing in court here does not contain a letter he stated in his testimony. So, what he presents as an illustration is different from the details of his evidence. State Attorney Mr. Saraji explained to the court that the objection of the Advocate Faraji was baseless, as they had already received a letter from a client requesting an investigation. "What we are handing over is a report of the results of an investigation conducted by a government chemist," said Mr. Saraji. He went on saying that the defense counsel did not indicate which section of the law was violated, as the objection must be in accordance with the law.

The learned Advocate Mr. Faraji replied that the witness had told the court that he had handed over to his supervisor the report of the inquiry procedure he had conducted to obtain the answers. The letter from the client—the police force—is not accompanied by the information provided here. The report is therefore incomplete. This is the reason for objecting the reception of this exhibit.

However, the court ruled that the defense counsel's objection was baseless as it did not specify any breach of the law and was therefore dismissed. Thus, the document containing the report of the results of the investigation dated 12 May 2020 was received in court as evidence number P2.

The first witness read illustration exhibit P2, "Within that figure of evidence; Exhibit A1 weighs 4.68 grams, Exhibit A2 weighs 4.50 grams, Exhibit A3 weighs 4.73 grams, Exhibit A4 weighs 4.62 grams, and Exhibit A5 weighs 4.87 grams. All together weigh 23.5 grams. All investigations carried out read well in the report." The witness continued, "when we receive the specimen, we have the sample indicator forms called GCLA 01, which we split the piece and inform the customer that we have received the specimen."

He said he could identify the form here, as it has his signature and registration number for the exhibit, which is SH LAB 132/2020. The witness was given documents and told the court that this was the sample indicator form. He said it has his signature and that he filled it out after receiving a sample from ASP Siame. It also has laboratory number 132/2020. He then asked the court to accept the sample form as an exhibit. The learned Advocate Faraji then told the court that he had no objection to that. The court received the document dated 12 May 2020, and marked it as Exhibit P3.

The court ordered the first witness to continue reading the P3 diagram. The Witness began by saying that the samples he received were pale white. He went on, "When I returned the samples, I packed them in a special bag using a stamp with the government chemist's logo. Each sample was in a nylon bag, and all together, I kept it in a large nylon bag. I can identify the bag because it was sealed with the government's chemist's logo."

The witness was given a bag; he identified it, and told the court that it was a nylon bag containing samples he had examined. "I have recognized it from its appearance and the logo of the government chemist on it, as well as my signature. I ask the court to accept this nylon bag as the exhibit I have been investigating."

Counsel Faraji objected to the receipt of the evidence in the absence of a receipt from the investigator. The lawyer quoted section 38 (3) of the Criminal Procedure Act No. 20 of 2019 which sets out how to conduct an investigation of seized controls. "They must give a receipt before the court, as proof that the samples examined have not been altered or destroyed," said Advocate Faraji, adding that the witness had stated his recourse to the sample and that the law required him as the investigator to submit a sample attached to the receipt. My Advocate insisted that it was the stand of the defense to see the receipt attached to the exhibit presented.

"This witness is the investigator; he has to hand over the receipt in court," Adv. Faraji further added that the exhibit shows that it was sealed by police officer badge number G2513 DC Ally, while according to the evidence presented by this witness, the sealant is unknown and is not mentioned anywhere in the statement. "I know that the exhibit can be submitted by anyone with full information or the developer. But the witness did not tell the court as to who parked this exhibit and neither did, he say who DC Ally was. The law requires a witness to give his testimony fluently and fully. This is not right at all."

According to Advocate Faraji, his statement is confirmed in the Criminal Procedure Code chapter 20 as amended in 2019, section 38 (3) and 48 (2) (c). The advocate continued, "It is very important to help the court to do justice. I, therefore, object to the receipt of this exhibit on the basis of the legal information I have submitted."

Following the objection of the Advocate Faraji, the State Attorney Mr. Saraji told the court that the learned Adv. Faraji has confused the issues of seizure control with what we have here in court. Mr. Saraji said, "Section 38 (1) refers to a police officer and not a witness from the chemist's office. So what lawyer Faraji is saying is not relevant here. And section 48 of the drug control and anti-drug law prescribes the form of arrest. Section 48 (2) (c) (viii) prescribes criminal arrest and controls.

The witness has not arrested the perpetrator or the authorities. The witness is here to prove that the controller exists as he closed it on 12 May 2020. He said that he received the bag from the police and, after completing the investigation, he closed it to return it to the police. So, the information provided by lawyer Faraji cannot take away the facts and proofs we have here." Mr. Saraji went on to advise Advocate Faraji to wait for those who conducted the search and seized exhibits to ask for the receipt matters. Mr. Saraji went on by saying that the presence of the name DC Ally is something that can be questioned. "So, the objection lacks legal grounds," concluded Mr. Saraji.

The learned Advocate Faraji told the court that he admits that the law he quoted refers to the arrest of the offender and the exhibit, but he has not mixed things up. His argument is that the evidence must be accompanied by a receipt. "This report does not have a receipt from the police or a government chemist. The receipt would prove to us that what was seized at the defendant's residence is what is presented here. The whole process must be clear and careful. Evidence also shows that DC Ally is the one who sealed this document. The witness was required to explain carefully and clearly, who had sealed the document. Due to the failure to provide sufficient evidence and numerous errors within the evidence he gives we are satisfied that this witness is not the right person to present this evidence. I, therefore, object the receipt of this evidence," said Adv. Faraji.

The court said that it had heard both sides' statements, and it was the court's opinion that the testimony given by this witness showed that he was well aware of the evidence he was presenting, so his presentation was correct. The magistrate reminded him of the DPP's case against Mizrai Pirbakhishi Hadija and three others, which is an appeal—criminal number 493/2016—Court of Appeal heard in Dar es Salaam. He told the lawyers to read in their private time.

With regard to the attachment of the receipt and the exhibit, the court found that Adv. Faraji's statement was related to the principle of arresting the offender and exhibits. So, sticking to the receipt in this statement is not important, and it is not appropriate at this stage. If the receipt carries the importance as stated by the defense advocate, then it must be submitted in accordance with the procedure prescribed by law and the witness responsible for the arrest of the accused and the exhibits. Regarding the existence of the name DC Ally as the person who sealed the exhibits as questioned by the learned advocate, the court found that the argument does not make this witness lack the dignity to present his evidence.

Therefore, the objections raised by the solicitor-general were dismissed with the nylon bag marked SH LAB No. 132/2020, those with bags are said to have drugs and were received and mark as Exhibit P4.

The first witness showed a sealed package, stated that it was the lab of a government chemist lab labeled GCLA, then read what was written in exhibit P4 and went on to explain, "The seal is as I closed it. It has my signature. If it had been played upon, it would not have been as it is and neither would my signature have been as it appears now."

Regarding the presence of a police force seal on the bag, the witness explained, "This is the mechanism the police force uses in delivering exhibits to the state chemist's laboratory. The person who sent the sample to the police does not have to send it to the state chemist. After receiving this sample from the police for investigation, I kept it with myself until I completed the investigation and handed it over to ASP Siame. The specimens I examined are in this nylon bag, which is received here as exhibit P4. I would like to open this document so that the illustrations I have examined can be seen."

The witness opened Exhibit P4. He said that this is how the samples he examined and proved to be Heroine Hydrochlorine. "I have identified them from the marks on each, which are A1 to A5. In Exhibit A1, there is a small bag which is what I did to determine the type of chemical and to measure its weight."

He went on, "I was convinced that these were Heroine Hydrochlorine drugs. I would like to open a small bag and another bag from inside to prove to the court that what is inside is powdered drug." The witness opened it and showed it to the court. He asked the court to accept the A1 mark as evidence. In his statement, the witness told the court that his investigation confirmed beyond a shadow of a doubt that the contents of the bag contained Heroin Hydrochloride. The witness then opened another slightly larger bag and showed it to the court. "This is the sample I have examined and I ask the court to accept it as evidence." The witness continued to open the bags marked A2, A3, A4, and A5, asking the court to accept each one as official exhibit in the court thereat.

When the witness finished testifying, Adv. Faraji stood to object the receipt of the exhibits as the witness had asked the court to accept what he said was powder. But what he is handing over is hard stuff; they are like pebbles, so Advocate Faraji objected to the receipt of the exhibits.

State Attorney Mr. Saraji responded to the objection by saying it lacked a legal basis. "The condition of the exhibits can be answered by a witness. There is receiving exhibits and measuring its weight. Here we discuss the receipt of the exhibits in the court. Receiving it is one thing, and inspecting it is another. The defense counsel did not comment on the reception. Witness testimony will help the court decide to review the evidence." Advocate Saraji continued, "The witness has explained how he conducted the examination of the samples he received and for that reason he has the status to hand over to the court here as exhibits. So, I ask the court to accept the exhibits!"

Advocate Faraji replied, "I did not say the exhibit has changed. The witness was required to state that he had received the flour and that it had now turned into pebbles. The fact is that the witness was sent flour and made into a flour test, but here he is asking for the pebbles to be received. He had to bring the flour he had investigated."

Then the magistrate said that he had listened carefully to the arguments of all parties, and there was no dispute that the witness received samples in the form of powder for investigation. "He identified them all, and in fact, he is brilliant and has the status to ask the court to receive the relevant exhibits as in the DPP's case against V. Mizrai, which I have quoted earlier." The magistrate went on to say, "Regarding the receipt of samples in the form of flour and now the samples have been brought to court as pebbles, those are matters that may be questioned in confirmation as the case progresses." Following the magistrate's explanation, the court dismissed the Consumer's objection and then five bags of heroin Hydrochloride and marked A1, A2, A3, A4, and A5 were received and re-marked P5, P6, P7, P8, and P9.

The Witness went on to explain that when he received the A1 to A5 illustrations, they were pale white. But now its color tends to be brown. "This drug was proven to be Heroine Hydrochloride. Like other chemicals, it can change color and texture. This means that they can change color and texture from powder to pebbles. These changes may be due to temperature or humidity. The nylon bag retains moisture naturally and can therefore cause these changes. It changes from a powder to a hard substance due to the effects by climate. The exhibit has changed slightly but has not yet become pebbles. They are large objects that can be crushed. The reason for this change is the humidity and temperature in the storage area."

***

After the state attorney has finished leading the first prosecution witness, cross-examination was followed between the defense counsel, Adv. Faraji Mangula, and the witness.

Adv. Mangula: *Remind us of your education and experience as a chemist.*

Witness Bilaro: *I am a graduate student in Environmental Sciences and Management.*

Adv. Mangula: *What profession do you have?*

Witness Bilaro: *I am a chemist.*

Adv. Mangula: *Who filled out the form for handing over the sample?*

Witness Bilaro: *ASP Siame filled out a form for sample submission and a state chemist form for receiving the sample.*

Adv. Mangula: *When did you receive the sample and the receipt form?*

Witness Bilaro: *I mentioned earlier that I received the form and the letter on 12 May 2020.*

Adv. Mangula: *During the examination of those samples in your laboratory, was the suspect or his lawyer present?*

Witness Bilaro: *Defendant was not present and his representative was also absent.*

Adv. Mangula: *Now, is there any oath to prove whether the investigation was actually carried out?*

Witness Bilaro: *I cannot make my own oath.*

Adv. Mangula: *While led by a state attorney, did you explain why you did not bring the materials used to investigate so that the court would not have doubts about the results?*

Witness Bilaro: *I did not state in my testimony that I would bring the results of the investigation I conducted and the materials I used in the investigation.*

Adv. Mangula: *How will the court believe that this investigation has taken place in your laboratory?*

Witness Bilaro: *The presence of a special seal we use in the office that we put in documents like this stands to be a great proof to that. This special seal is proof that the work has been done in our office.*

Adv. Mangula: *Witness! Who was on duty that day when the police brought Samples to the office?*

Witness Bilaro: *The police came and found me on duty that day.*

Adv. Mangula gave the Witness Exhibit P1, which is the form of handover and after giving it he went on to ask him,

Adv. Mangula: *Witness, is this document special or not special?*

Witness Bilaro: *This document does not come from our office, so I do not know if it is special or not.*

Adv. Mangula: *Does this document you said come from the police have a seal to prove that it is from the police?*

Witness Bilaro: *No, it has no seal.*

Adv. Mangula: *Now why did you receive it despite having that deficiency?*

Witness Bilaro: *I received it because I was a chemist on duty. When the police arrived at the office, they found me on duty.*

Adv. Mangula: *You said this form does not have a police seal, does it have the seal or logo of your office?*

Witness Bilaro: *The form does not have our office seal or logo.*

Adv. Mangula: *Why?*

Witness Bilaro: *Because this form does not come from our office.*

Adv. Mangula: *Who signed the form?*

Witness Bilaro: *The form was signed by the person who brought the sample to the office and I as a recipient.*

Adv. Mangula: *What evidence is there that the form was received at your office?*

Witness Bilaro: *The form filled at the time of receipt of the sample was stamped on our seal and that is the proof that it came from us.*

Adv. Mangula: *Can you show the court the form?*

Witness Bilaro: *The form is not here in court.*

Adv. Mangula: *The suspect was arrested here in Mbeya, and your offices are here in Mbeya, why did you not go to investigate the suspect's home where it is said that samples were found?*

Witness Bilaro: *The process of conducting an investigation is taking place in a laboratory. It would not have been possible to conduct any investigation in the area where the samples were seized. We use hazardous chemicals in research. I need special protective equipment.*

Adv. Mangula handed the Witness Exhibit P2, then proceeded to question him.

Adv. Mangula: *Please show on this exhibit where the defendant; has signed.*

Witness Bilaro: *This statement has not been signed by the defendant; it has been signed by my supervisor.*

Adv. Mangula: *Is there any place on this exhibit that indicates the position of the sample holder?*

Witness Bilaro: *The other documents do not indicate the rank of investigator. It just shows work.*

Adv. Mangula: *Where did the defendant's representative sign on this document?*

Witness Bilaro: *This statement is not signed by the defendant's representative.*

Adv. Mangula: *Why does it not have the signature of the defendant's representative?*

Witness Bilaro: *This is our procedure.*

Adv. Mangula: *How will the court believe if this document comes from your office?*

Witness Bilaro: *This document is from our office, which is why it has been signed by officials from our office.*

The Witness was given Exhibit P3, and cross-examination continued.

Adv. Mangula: *When you were led by a state attorney, you talked about one form having a seal and the other not having a seal?*

Witness Bilaro: *I did not say in my testimony why one document is sealed and the other does not.*

Adv. Mangula: *But do you agree with me that all these documents come from your office?*

Witness Bilaro: *It is true that all these documents come from our office.*

The Witness was given a P4 model, a nylon bag containing five small drug paraphernalia, and the interrogation continued.

Adv. Mangula: *Were you a witness or were you present when the accused was arrested with the samples you examined?*

Witness Bilaro: *I did not participate in the capture of the model I came to investigate.*

Adv. Mangula: *Do you know how they were seized?*

Witness Bilaro: *I do not know how they were seized.*

Adv. Mangula: *The specimens brought to court are pale white. Now how will the court believe if these specimens are the seized samples?*

Witness Bilaro: *There is nothing in this court that is pale white.*

Adv. Mangula: *And what color is this?* Adv. Mangula asked as he showed the bag of samples.

Witness Bilaro: *The pale color is a pale white.*

Adv. Mangula: *I ask you again what color is this.*

Witness Bilaro: *This color in the exhibit is not pale white.*

Adv. Mangula: *Do you agree with me that there is a difference between the flour and this that is present here in the court?*

Witness Bilaro: *Of course, there is a difference between the powder and the condition of the samples now.*

Adv. Mangula: *In your statement filed here in court, did you mention about that difference?*

Witness Bilaro: *In my statement, I did not show the difference between the sample received and the current one.*

Adv. Mangula: *Since you have admitted that you did not explain any sample differences between what was received and what is here now, did you take an oath to explain about that difference?*

Witness Bilaro: *I did not take an oath to explain the nature and color of the exhibit.*

Adv. Mangula: *Now with that information, how will the court believe if this model has not been tampered with or changed?*

Witness Bilaro: *In the testimony I gave here, I explained the security issues in Exhibit P4. The bags were undamaged, and that they had numbers.*

Adv. Mangula: *This exhibit containing the sample shows who was responsible for sealing it?*

Witness Bilaro: *The envelope shows that it was closed by DC Ally.*

Adv. Mangula: *Why was it sealed by DC Ally?*

Witness Bilaro: *I have already told the court why he sealed it.*

Adv. Mangula: *When were they sealed?*

Witness Bilaro: *All seals were put on 12 May 2020. Ally put a police seal. I put seal for a state chemist's office.*

Adv. Mangula: *Are these the specimens you researched?*

Witness Bilaro: *Yes, these are the specimens I received for further investigation.*

Adv. Mangula: *How were they?*

Witness Bilaro: *They were in powder form.*

Adv. Mangula: *What is the condition the chemicals you use in your investigation?*

Witness Bilaro: *The chemical used for examination is in a liquid form.*

Adv. Mangula: *What is the condition of the reagent you are using?*

Witness Bilaro: *The reagents are in liquid form.*

Adv. Mangula: *Can the reagents change the nature of the material?*

Witness Bilaro: *I do not know if the reagents can change the material.*

Adv. Mangula: *Explain to the court, how you conducted your investigation?*

Witness Bilaro: *I started by measuring the weight of the exhibit first. I took 0.5 grams from each sample for testing.*

The witness was given exhibit P2, which is a chemist's report.

Adv. Mangula continued to question the witness:

Adv. Mangula: *You said that you took 0.5 grams from each bag containing the sample, so how many grams of samples remained in total?*

Witness Bilaro: *By removing 0.5 grams from each bag, it means that the weight of the entire exhibit together would remain 20.90 grams.*

Adv. Mangula: *Now the accused is said to have been found to be 23.4 grams, but here in the court, you have brought samples of 20.90 grams. In your statement filed here in court, did you write down the reasons that led to the difference in that weight?*

Witness Bilaro: *A reduction of 0.5 grams in each exhibit was not in my statement.*

Adv. Mangula: *Have you seen the charge sheet?*

Witness Bilaro: *I have never seen a charge sheet in this case.*

Adv. Mangula then completed his cross-examination and returned to his seat.

After being cross-examined by the defense counsel, the first witness for the republic was corrected by a state attorney.

After correction, he was released from the dock, and the court was silent for a while.

The state's attorney told the court that the prosecution had other witnesses and it was now at six o'clock in the evening. "Please let us continue tomorrow. Due to its sensitivity, I request this court to seal the P5, P6, P7, P8, and P9 and hand them over to the police officers for protection, in order to ensure the security of the model and that it will not be tampered with or lost."

Adv. Mangula says he had no objection.

The court accepted the attorney's request and ordered that the clerk of the court stamp the envelope, seal it, and hand it over to the police officer in writing. When the exhibits are brought to court again, they will be presented to the state attorney and the defense attorney.

***

The trial resumed on 2 December 2020 before the Resident Magistrate Hon. Z. D Laizer. The court hearing was attended by state attorneys Mr. Saraji Iboru, Mrs. Prosista, and Mr. Davice. I was personally present with my lawyer, Learned Adv. Mangula, and court the clerk was Ms. Luce.

After the lawyers from both sides expressed their presence, the session continued by bringing in the second prosecution witness, this was ASP Sylvester Clement Siame, thirty-eight, a Christian, a police officer living in the Sabasaba area of Mbeya region.

Interviewed by State Counsel, the second witness for the prosecution—PW2, stated that he is a police officer and that he worked in the Mbeya's RCO office as an assistant to the RCO. "I have been in this office since 2018. My responsibilities are to investigate and as an RCO assistant, I supervise police officers, arrest criminals and conduct criminal investigations. I also oversee the follow-up of police officers' shifts." Regarding his education, the witness stated that he has a bachelor's degree in law from Hope University, from which he graduated in 2009. He said he is currently pursuing a bachelor's degree in Security and Intelligence in China.

The State Attorney asked the witness to explain where he was on 9 May 2020 and what happened.

The Witness replied, "On 9 May 2020, at eleven o'clock in the morning, I was home. Mbeya RCO ACP Andrew Kantimbo called me on the phone and told me to go to the office urgently as there was an urgent matter to take care of. When I arrived at his office, he told me that there was a man called Mdude Nyagali spreading false information and incitement against the government led by Hon. President John Joseph Magufuli with the aim of inciting the people too hate the president and his government. Therefore, he should be arrested immediately."

"He also called Inspector Joram from the cybercrime department and two other officers; DC Edger and DC Said. We were all together given the task to make sure that we arrest Mdude. Our search for him over the Internet was unsuccessful that day. We continued with the search for him the on next day and then we received information from our informant that Mdude will be in the CHADEMA offices located in Kadege area. We set a trap there. When evening came, we saw him coming down from the 'bajaj.'"

The state's attorney asked the witness if the procedures for arresting the suspect were followed. The witness said, "I followed him and introduced myself by my name and title and explained to him on his mistakes. I told him that he was accused of spreading false and hateful information through social media and asked him to accompany us to the RCO Mbeya office.

He agreed to accompany us to the office for the RCO. Upon my arrival, I instructed Inspector Joram to take his statement on the charges against him. Shortly afterwards, Joram returned to me and informed me that the defendant had refused to provide any information until his lawyer was present. I instructed Joram to find his lawyer and while the lawyer is being sought, then the suspect should be remanded in custody at the Central Station of Mbeya."

The state's attorney asked the witness to explain what happened after the defendant refused to write a statement.

The witness explained, "On 11 May 2020, in the morning, a man by the name of Fadhili came to the office and introduced himself as Mdude's lawyer. He explained that he had come to see his client, who is Mdude. I told him that his client was in custody at the Central Station and that he was waiting for him to witness the interrogation. When the lawyer arrived at the station, Mdude agreed to be interrogated."

The Witness went on to explain, "We suggested that before interviewing him we should go to his house for a search. I led the caravan with Corporal Charles and Advocate Fadhili. Suspect Mdude led us to him where we went on a police force car. We asked him about his ten-house member and he told us he was there. We searched for the telephone number of this cell leader who was called John, and called him and he immediately came to Mdude's residence. We told him that we have come to search Mdude's house as he was suspected of spreading false and hateful information through social media."

The state attorney asked if legal procedures were followed during the search.

The Witness replied, "Legal procedures were followed as I told Mdude to search us first, beginning with me and then Corporal Charles, then lawyer Fadhili and cell leader John. We did not find anyone at Mdude's residence. Since we had a cell leader, we started a search while he was witnessing. His house was locked and Mdude himself unlocked the door of his house. After opening the door, the search started in his bedroom. In that room, we found two Nokia and Samsung phones and one Tigo line. We went to another room but found nothing among what we needed. We went to the living room where we found twenty-four CDs, which we took with us. On the TV table, we found an envelope of khaki with two nylon bags in it. I called Mdude and told him do you see this? And he answered me yes. I told him that this powder is believed to be a drug. But we will be satisfied after being tested by a state chemist to also find out what kind of drugs was it."

The Witness went on to explain, "The drugs were hidden under the couch. There were two bags. After opening it, we found five bags of flour that had a pale white color. After that, we filled out Form No. 3 from the Drug Control Authority to prove that we have seized an exhibit. After filling out the form, we all signed. I can identify the form because it has my signature."

After the explanation, the witness was given the documents, and he recognized it as Form No. 3 drug seizures. He asked the court to accept the document as an example. Advocate Faraji said he had no objection to that.

The second witness went on to tell the court that, "The independent witness who witnessed the search was Mr. John L Mwanyumba as read on the form. The lawyer for the accused Mr. Fadhili M. Shombe as shown on the form. The person being searched is Mdude M. Nyagali. In a search, we found the drug in five bundles in nylon bags that were placed inside a khaki envelope. We also found one black Nokia phone and another black Samsung phone. We also found one Tigo line and about twenty CDs, we took all those goods with us."

The state attorney wanted to know what happened after the search.

The witness went on with more explanations, "After the search, we headed to the Mbeya RCO's office for further legal action. Upon arrival at the office, I handed over the samples to the person in charge, DC Ally. The suspect was present and witnessed me handing over the exhibits to DC Ally. I filled out a form for the prescription and finally asked Corporal Charles to interview Mdude about his alleged drug addiction. Regarding the allegations of spreading false information through social media, I gave the task to Inspector Joram."

The witness continued, "On 12 May 2020, I ordered the suspect to be brought to my office from the Mbeya Central Police Station. When he arrived at my office, I told him that we would close the sample to be sent to a state chemist for investigation. We called a free witness, Mrs. Semeni, to witness the sealing of the exhibit in front of the suspect. DC Ally brought the exhibit we showed the suspect the day before. The samples were marked A1, A2, A3, A4, and A5. Each exhibit was inside a nylon bag. Each bag was placed in one exhibit bag, and each bag was marked with the same marks A1, A2, A3, A4, and A5. I ordered a statement from an independent witness who witnessed the sealing of these exhibits. I handed the specimens for submission to the state chemist. At the time, the suspect was remanded in custody."

The witness continued, "I went to the government chemist's offices located in Iwambi area. I found a Chemist named Bilaro who is the first witness, I had a Form No. 1 of the Drug Control Authority, and I also had a model that was thought to be a drug. I also had a letter of introduction to a government chemist. Form No. 1 is for sending samples to a chemist for examination."

The prosecutor asked the witness how he could identify the form.

The Witness replied, "I can identify the form because I filled it in myself and it has my signature."

The witness was given Exhibit P1. He identified it as the form No.1 by showing his signature along with the signature of chemist Jansen Bilaro on it.

The witness continued, "The chemist started examining the specimens given to him by me and gave me results that all the specimens are Heroine and its total weight is 23.4 Grams. He then sealed it and prepared a statement for his post as a 'government chemist.'"

The state's attorney asked the witness to explain what happened after the chemist completed the investigation.

The Witness replied, "He gave me the exhibit and the information and I took it to the office, where I handed it over to DC Ally for safekeeping."

The state attorney asked him if he could identify the information given to him by the Chemist. The witness replied that he could identify the information he had been given because he had read it and it had been signed by Bilaro.

The State Attorney presented the witness with Exhibit P2. The witness identified it as the chemist's statement. He said, "It has Bilaro's signature. I received it on 12 May, 2020. I was also given a letter confirming that they had received the sample."

The State Attorney provided the witness with Exhibit P3. The witness recognized it and stated that the form was the one he had signed after handing over the sample to the chemist. "This form confirms that they have received a sample suspected of being a drug. I can also identify the sample envelope as it is inside a nylon bag and has Bilaro's signature. It's a bag through which one can see what's inside."

The State Attorney provided the witness with P4 figure. The witness said the envelope was a sample handed to him by chemist Bilaro. In it, there are drugs. "This package contains the exhibits marked A1, A2, A3, A4, and A5. They all contain flour, which is a drug. This is the same pattern I was given by a chemist after examining it. There is a long and careful process in transfer exhibit from one person to another. The first handover was from me to DC Ally and the second was from me to Chemist Bilaro. The form has my signature."

The witness was then given a document, which he identified and stated that this indicates that chain of custody on the handover of the exhibit was well followed. The witness asked the court to accept the document as an exhibit in the ongoing case. Advocate Faraji had no objection. The Court received the exhibit dated 11 May 2020 as an Exhibit P11.

The second witness reading Exh. P11 went stating that, according to this form on 11 May 2020 there was a handover between him and DC Ally. On 12 May 2020, the handover took place between DC Ally and himself, and then handed over to Chemist Bilaro. Bilaro then handed it over to him, and he handed it to DC Ally.

The prosecutor asked the witness if he could identify me as a defendant. The witness said he could identify me. "Here he is on the dock," said the witness.

After an interview with the state attorney and the second prosecution witness, it was followed by the defense counsel's cross-examination.

Adv. Mangula: *When the state attorney led, you said you had a law degree. Is it true?*

Witness Siame: *It is true. I am a lawyer because I have a law degree.*

Adv. Mangula: *Are you a leaned advocate?*

Witness Siame: *I am not.*

Adv. Mangula: *So here, I am talking to someone who is knowledgeable enough about legal issues?*

Witness Siame: *I am currently pursuing my postgraduate studies. I have a very good understanding of the law.*

The witness went on to say that although the state attorney did not ask him about his working experience, he only asked to tell the court that he has seventeen years of experience as a detective.

Adv. Mangula: *Do you know the legal procedures for arresting suspects?*

Witness Siame: *I know the procedures to be followed in arresting a suspect and taking him to the police station.*

Adv. Mangula: *Do you know the rules and procedures to be followed by police, I mean Police General Orders (PGO)?*

Witness Siame: *I am aware of the Police Code of Conduct. These PGO are the laws that guide us in carrying out our duties as police officers. We must follow them.*

Adv. Mangula: *Tell the court after arresting the suspect where did you take him to?*

Witness Siame: *After his arrest, we took the suspect to the office of the RCO.*

Adv. Mangula: *So, you did not send him into custody?*

Witness Siame: *He was not remanded in custody. He was later remanded in custody under my instructions to Inspector Joram.*

Adv. Mangula: *Is there any evidence that the accused was remanded in custody?*

Witness Siame: *There is an inmate register.*

Adv. Mangula: *You say you sent someone. Do you know anything that was going on in remand?*

Witness Siame: *Unfortunately, I do not know what happened in custody.*

Adv. Mangula: *What information is included in that inmate register?*

Witness Siame: *Details of the accused, about his health, allegations against him, and who issued his arrest warrant are included in the detainee's register.*

Adv. Mangula: *Are the defendant's property information also registered there on the register?*

Witness Siame: *A statement of the property and equipment belonging to the suspect is kept in the asset register or PPR.*

Adv. Mangula: *What are the defendant's assets recorded in that register or PPR?*

Witness Siame: *I do not know if there was anything recorded there because I was not personally present during the exercise.*

Adv. Mangula: *When you arrested the suspect did, he has the keys to his house?*

Witness Siame: *Yes.*

Adv. Mangula: *Who had the keys to the defendant's house?*

Witness Siame: *I said the keys were with the suspect himself.*

Adv. Mangula: *Is the accused allowed to enter custody with his keys?*

Witness Siame: Advocate *No. The suspect is not allowed to enter with his keys in custody. Instead, the keys and other assets are registered in the register and kept by the police officer on duty.*

Adv. Mangula: *Show the court a register showing the assets of the accused that he handed over before he was remanded in custody.*

Witness Siame: *I cannot show the register as it is not here in court.*

Adv. Mangula: *If I say that you police officers seized the suspect's property including the keys to his house without recording it in the register would I be right?*

Witness Siame: *You will not be right.*

Adv. Mangula: *If I say, you held the suspect's properties including the keys to his house even after the accused was released from custody, would I be right?*

Witness Siame: *That is not true, as the accused was not granted bail. 'When the accused is released from custody, he will be given PPR and when he returns, he will be given another PPR.*

Adv. Mangula: *Are you aware that Mdude is a member of CHADEMA?*

Witness Siame: *Yes, I know that the accused is a member of CHADEMA.*

Adv. Mangula: *Would I be right to say that you arrested Mdude for political reasons due to his CHADEMA membership?*

Witness Siame: *All I know is that Mdude has been arrested on charges of publishing online false and hateful statements against President Magufuli.*

Adv. Mangula: *Are you aware that Mdude has been repeatedly accused of publishing false information on social media?*

Witness: *I do not know.*

Adv. Mangula: *Do you know that Mdude has been abducted and tortured?*

Witness Siame: *I do not know.*

Adv. Mangula: *Do you agree with me that Magufuli is a member of CCM?*

Witness Siame: *'It is true that Magufuli is a member of CCM.*

Adv. Mangula: *Are you aware that CHADEMA is vying for power just like CCM?*

Witness Siame: *Yes, I know.*

Adv. Mangula *Are you aware that in the contest for power CHADEMA members and leaders have been arrested, tortured and abducted including Mdude?*

Witness Siame: *I do not know if CCM and CHADEMA have such animosity. As far as I know these are just competing for leadership and not for the faint of heart.*

Adv. Mangula: *Will you agree with me that you conducted a search just one day after arresting the suspect?*

Witness Siame: *It is true that we conducted a search at the suspect's residence a day after his arrest.*

Adv. Mangula: *Who had the keys to the suspect's house before the search?*

Witness Siame: *He had the keys to the house himself, although he did not take them into custody.*

Adv. Mangula: *Before evicting him and going to search his house, was the suspect ever remanded in custody?*

Witness Siame: *The suspect was immediately released from custody and went to be searched at his home.*

Adv. Mangula: *When you released him from custody, did you question the PPR in order to be satisfied with the handover of the defendant's properties?*

Witness Siame: *I really did not ask for the PPR form, as it was not important to me at the time.*

Adv. Mangula: *Who participated as an independent witness during the search?*

Witness Siame: *We received a great deal of cooperation from a government official who witnessed the whole operation.*

Adv. Mangula: *Do you know that the person you are identifying as an independent witness is not a government official but a member of CCM?*

Witness Siame: *I do not know.*

Adv. Mangula: *Who led the search operation?*

Witness Siame: *I personally led the exercise.*

Adv. Mangula: *How did you find that independent witness and how did you know he was a government official?*

Witness Siame: *We identified him as a member of the government after questioning the suspect's neighbors.*

Adv. Mangula: *Who entered the house for a search?*

Witness Siame: *The entrants of the house are Corporal Charles, Fadhili, John and the accused himself.*

Adv. Mangula: *Tell the court how you conducted the search.*

Witness Siame: *After entering, we closed the door. The search began in the bedroom of the suspect.*

Adv. Mangula: *Is it a legal requirement to search from the closet?*

Witness Siame: *Basically, a search can start anywhere.*

Adv. Mangula: *Is there any law that prevents a defendant from interfering in a search operation if he or she does not see it fit?*

Witness Siame: *The accused may intervene in the search operation to help find the required results. But in this case, the accused had no choice but to decide who should not enter his house.*

Adv. Mangula: *In your investigation you found out the suspect has any history of drug use?*

Witness Siame: *I do not know.*

Adv. Mangula: *In your knowledge, a local government leader from a political party can be an independent witness?*

Witness Siame: *The local government leader is an independent witness to the search. He may not be a member of any political party.*

Adv. Mangula handed the witness Exhibit P10 and then proceeded to question the witness.

Adv. Mangula: *Where was this document signed?*

Witness Siame: *This document was signed at the scene.*

Adv. Mangula: *Why does this document not have the seal of the signed members?*

Witness Siame: (witness remained silent)

Adv. Mangula told the witness to read the document carefully. There is a dot between the first and second entries. One number has been deleted and two numbers have also been deleted. Only design objects remain. Then Adv. Mangula continued to question the witness.

Adv. Mangula: *Who gave you the name of the alleged member of the ten houses?*

Witness Siame: *The accused himself gave us the name of his ten-member leader of the houses.*

Adv. Mangula: *Were you able to identify the member by his or her identity?*

Witness Siame: *We did not ask for the cell leader's ID. However, there was another witness who is Advocate Fadhili Shombe.*

Adv. Mangula: *Will you agree with me that the weight of the sample allegedly found in the suspect's home is different from the weight presented here in court?*

Witness Siame: *Yes, the weight stated in court is not the same as that given in the exhibit.*

After the answer, Adv. Mangula handed the charge sheet to the Prosecution witness, showed him where to read and then proceeded with the questions.

Adv. Mangula: *Read here, how is it written?*
Witness Siame: *Drug Trafficking.*
Adv. Mangula: *Now tell the court where Mdude was transporting drugs from and to what destination.*
Witness Siame: Silence.

After a short silence, the magistrate asked the witness to answer the question. The Witness asked for water, and it was given to him.

Witness Siame (after drinking water): *You know that the drugs the suspect was found with are not produced in Tanzania; they are from Pakistan and Afghanistan.*

Adv. Mangula: *So, you want to say Mdude has come out with it from Pakistan and Afghanistan?*

Witness Siame: *It is possible.*

Adv. Mangula: *Mdude does not have a passport now! How did he get to Pakistan and Afghanistan and what method did he use to smuggle drugs into Tanzania?*

Witness Siame: *The suspect knows for himself what method he used to smuggle the drugs into the country from Pakistan and Afghanistan.*

Adv. Mangula: *And you are a seventeen years, working as detective specializing in drug trafficking but you cannot establish how the suspect Mdude smuggled drugs from Pakistan to Tanzania?*

Witness Siame: *Yes.*

Then Adv. Mangula gave the witness exhibit P11—that is a form of chain of custody—and asked him if the suspect is part of the handover.

Witness Siame: *The accused was not part of the handover.*

Adv. Mangula: *When you went to the suspect's house to conduct a search how many vehicles did you have?*

Witness Siame: *We left together in a police force's Land Cruiser on the way to the suspect's home.*

Adv. Mangula: *Defendant is a tenant, is he? When you got to his residence; did you find the landlord?*

Witness Siame: *I do not remember.*

Adv. Mangula: *Since you were planning to conduct a search, did you put security at the suspect's house while the suspect was in custody?*

Witness Siame: *We did not allocate any guard, as we did not know where the suspect lived.*

Adv. Mangula: *Do you know if Mdude has filed a lawsuit against your boss Inspector General Police – IGP Sirro?*

Witness Siame: *I do not know.*

Adv. Mangula gives witness Siame Exhibit P4—that is a nylon bag carrying five bags of samples—and then proceeded to question him.

Adv. Mangula: *How did you know the samples allegedly arrested at the suspect's home where drugs before even laboratory examination was conducted?*

Witness Siame: *I have worked at the headquarters of the drug control authority for over 10 years. So, I was able to identify the drugs just by looking. When I saw this powder, I suspected it was a drug.*

Adv. Mangula: *Tell the court where you sent the samples you claim are drugs after finding them at the suspect's home.*

Witness Siame: *After seizing these drugs, we took them to the office to the RCO.*

Adv. Mangula: *Who was the custodian of those exhibits?*

Witness Siame: *The illustrator was DC Ally who sealed and marked these exhibits.*

Adv. Mangula: *Who witnessed the sealing and marking of such exhibits?*

Witness Siame: *they were marked in front of the accused and me as well.*

Adv. Mangula: *Do you have any knowledge of the application of criminal law, I mean Criminal Proceeding Act (CPA)?*

Witness Siame: *I know what it says but I do not use it often.*

Adv. Mangula: *Tell the court, what color these samples look?*

Witness Siame: *All exhibits show that it is a pale white powder.*

Adv. Mangula: *Were you present when the chemist testified in court?*

Witness Siame: *No, I was not.*

Adv. Mangula: *Were you present when the sample bag was closed by the chemist?*

Witness Siame: *Yes.*

Adv. Mangula: *Do you agree with me that DC Ally is the one who sealed the exhibit bag?*

Witness Siame: *DC Ally is not the one who sealed the exhibit bag.*

Adv. Mangula: *Do you know Ms. Semeni who was a free witness at the time of packing the sample for the chemist?*

Witness Siame: *I do not know her; I have no information about that witness.*

Adv. Mangula: *You said Mdude was accused of insulting President Magufuli. Has the president himself complained?*

Witness Siame: *I don't know if the President has ever complained?*

Adv. Mangula: *Are the offenses of publishing false or defamatory statements bailable?*

Witness Siame: *Yes, they have bail.*

Adv. Mangula: *Are these drug trafficking charges he is currently accused of, bailable?*

Witness Siame: *To this drug charge, bail is not guaranteed especially for the amount as seized from this suspect.*

Adv. Mangula: *Why did you not take the witness of the accused Mr. Fadhili Shombe with you to the station after the search?*

Witness Siame: *The car we had was small; it did not have enough space for all the passengers.*

Adv. Mangula handed the witness exhibit P1, which is a letter of identification from the police to the chemist and questions, continued.

Adv. Mangula: *This P1 exhibit has no seal. I mean that this is not a real letter. Now where is the real letter?*

Witness Siame: *I do not know where it is.*

Adv. Mangula then asked the witness to explain to the court the methods they used to find the suspect and arrest him. The witness said that the suspect was not reachable through his phone and they did not consider asking for him to his party leaders. After that interview, re-examination followed as led by State Attorney Mr. Davice Saraji to Witness Siame.

***

The third Prosecution Witness was G2513 DC Ally, a thirty-two-year-old, Muslim, resident of Ituha. He took an oath before the court that he would tell the truth in the evidence he will give.

Giving evidence before the court, DC Ally said he is working as a Detective Officer. State Attorney Mr. Saraji asked the witness to explain his duties and responsibilities. Witness Ally said, "My job is to investigate crimes, arrest criminals, and be responsible for storing specimens in the RCO office. So, I take care of the keys to the special storage room."

The State Attorney continued to lead witness Ally, wanting to explain where he was and what his responsibilities were on 11 May 2020. The witness told the court that on 11 May 2020, at four-thirty in the evening, he was continuing to work as usual in his office. The Witness went on to say, "I was called by ASP Siame, and he gave me specimen for storage. The specimens were powder that was suspected to be drugs. It was five bags that were wrapped in a nylon bag that was placed inside a khaki envelope. I was also handed 1 Tigo line, a Nokia phone, and 20 CDs. I received the sample and stored them in a special box at FFU Mbeya."

Witness Ally continued, "On 12 May 2020, at eight o'clock in the evening, I took a sample from our box and sent it to the RCO Mbeya office. After that, I put a mark on the exhibits, which are A1, A2, A3, A4, and A5. I did all this in front of witnesses in the presence of the suspect who was arrested on this charge."

The State Attorney asked Witness Ally to testify as to who were present at the sealing and marking of the exhibits. The Witness replied, "Those who witnessed the sealing were ASP Siame, F4656 DC Charles, and Sakina, who was an independent witness. After that, I packed all specimens in a nylon bag and handed it over to ASP Siame, who sent it to a government chemist."

The witness continued, "On the 12 May 2020, in the evening, I received these exhibits again from ASP Siame. But at this time, they had a note from the state chemist. I wrote a note of this handover in a special register and finally went to store it in our box in the FFU Mbeya office."

"On 1st December 2020, I removed these exhibits from our box at FFU Mbeya and brought them to the court on the day the state chemist was required to testify before this court."

The State Attorney asked the witness to explain more about the preservation of the exhibits and the dates he had kept since receiving them.

The Witness continued to explain, "The specimens are under the RCO. But in reality, it is I who keeps it. I kept the keys from the first day until 1 December 2020. The first entry for these exhibits was 11 May 2020."

State Attorney Mr. Saraji asked the witness if he could identify the register and the specimen he mentioned at the beginning.

The Witness replied, "I can identify the relevant register because it has my handwriting and my force number. I can identify the exhibit because I myself marked them as A1, A2, A3, A4, and A5. The evidentiary package contains the stamp of a state chemist. I closed the exhibition bag and handed it over to ASP Siame."

Witness was given Exhibit no. P4. He recognized it and said that this was the envelope he had sealed. He said it has a government approval. The witness identified one packet after another from A1 to A5 and told the court that he had sealed the exhibits himself and put them in a witness bag.

The witness went on to explain before the court that there was a special handover form that he had filled out for identification of these exhibits. The witness was given Exhibit number P10 and identified it. He told the court that the form had his name, force number, and signature. "The handover took place between me and ASP Siame on 11 May 2020, and the next day on 12 May 2020, the sample was handed to me by ASP Siame."

The witness continued, "I received this document on 11 May 2020, and kept it for court use. I also put my signature in the court records register." The register was handed over to the court and marked P12, and asked by the court to receive it as an important exhibit.

After the chief examination by State Attorney to the Third Witness, the time came for Defense Advocate Mangula to take cross-examination against the third witness, DC Ally.

Adv. Mangula: *Witness! Remind us about your education.*

Witness Ally: *I have a University degree in ICT from UDOM.*

Adv. Mangula: *What year did you graduate and join the police force?*

Witness Ally: *I graduated in 2015, and joined the police force in 2009.*

Adv. Mangula: *When ASP Siame handed you the sample at the RCO office, did you record it anywhere?*

Witness Ally: *I did not record the exhibit anywhere because the envelope he handed to me was open.*

Adv. Mangula handed the witness Exhibit P4, which is a bag containing five bags of flour, and Exhibit P9, which is one of the bags containing the flour. Questions continue.

Adv. Mangula: *Who sealed these exhibits?*

Witness Ally: *I sealed exhibit P4.*

Adv. Mangula: *Where is the alleged khaki envelope found in the suspect's residence?*

Witness Ally: *The envelope I received from ASP Siame is not here.*

Adv. Mangula: *When you were led by a state attorney, you said where is the envelope?*

Witness Ally: *I did not say where the envelope is but what I said was that the envelope is not here.*

Adv. Mangula: *Was the suspect present when you marked the exhibit?*

Witness Ally: *I marked A1 to A5 in front of the suspect.*

Adv. Mangula: *Did any of the accused's relatives witnessed or sign?*

Witness Ally: *No relative of the accused has signed the seal of this exhibit.*

Adv. Mangula: *Is there any indication as to whether the powder handed over to ASP Siame is the same sent to the chemist?*

Witness Ally: *The flour inside these bags has not been marked.*

Adv. Mangula: *Is there any DNA information in these exhibits?*

Witness Ally: *There was no DNA information about these exhibits.*

The witness is given an exhibit number P12, which is the exhibition register at the RCO office, and identifies the exhibit as the register he filled out when he received the specimens. He said, "There are reports of seized equipment which are suspected drugs, one Tigo line, a Nokia phone, and about twenty CDs."

Adv. Mangula: *The Khaki envelope allegedly to be found with drugs in the suspect's home is among the assets in the register?*

Witness Ally: *No.*

Adv. Mangula: *Where is that envelope, or is it here in court?*

Witness Ally: *The envelope has not been brought to court; it is at the police station.*

Advocate Mangula: *Did you do a DNA test or fingerprint to identify who held the envelope and placed it at the suspect's home?*

Witness Ally: *We did not.*

Adv. Mangula: *Would you agree with me that a DNA test on the envelope is necessary to identify the holder?*

Witness Ally: *It is true that the test can show who touched the specimen before.*

Adv. Mangula: *Why didn't you send an actual envelope that was allegedly found with drugs at the suspect's residence?*

Witness Ally: *I used the handover bag instead of the envelope that contained these specimens because it was held by so many people.*

Adv. Mangula: *Do you agree with me that DNA tests and fingerprints would bring real answers and help the court?*

Witness Ally: *Examination in the envelope would not bring true answers.*

Adv. Mangula: *Who was the last to seal this exhibit* (while showing Exhibit P4).

Witness Ally: *The last person to seal this bag is the government chemist.*

Adv. Mangula: *You were not responsible for sealing this exhibit?*

Witness Ally: *I sealed it before it was sent to a chemist.*

Adv. Mangula: *Remind the court who was the independent witness when you sealed this bag.*

Witness Ally: *The witness present is known as Sakina Ally or Semeni. She is my mother.*

Adv. Mangula: *Prior to the submission of the exhibits, did you have any information on the arrest of the suspect?*

Witness Ally: *I had no information about the arrest of the suspect. What I received is just a specimen.*

Adv. Mangula: *When you received the exhibits A1 to A5 in what color were they?*

Witness Ally: *They were pale white.*

Adv. Mangula: *Is this a pale white color?* (While showing the sample bag)

Witness Ally: *Today they have turned brown.*

Adv. Mangula: *When the state attorney led you, did you explain this color difference?*

Witness Ally: *When I was interviewed by the state attorney, I did not mention this color difference.*

The state attorney Mr. Davice intervened in the interview and told the court that it is only a chemist who could explain the differences in these colors. The magistrate asked Advocate Mangula to continue, but Adv. Mangula claimed to have finish his examination.

The state attorney asked the court to set another date for the continuation of the hearing. He also requested that the exhibits be kept at the custody of police, as was the order from yesterday.

Adv. Mangula had no objection to that request.

The court ordered that specimens P4 to P9 be kept as ordered on 1 December 2020, and immediately ordered that another hearing be held on 3 December 2020. However, the prosecution did not produce witnesses on the 3 December, so the court adjourned the hearing to 22 December 2020.

***

I was again arraigned before the Mbeya Resident Magistrate's Court on December 22, 2020, but my Advocate Mr. Faraji Mangula did not appear before the court and on instead sent a representative, Mr. Philip Mwakilima. However, due to the argument of the Defense Advocate Mr. Mwakilima, that he did not have any instructions on this case to be heard, so he asked the court to reschedule the case to 5 January 2021, if the court calendar allows.

The state attorney told the court that he had no objection to the request. The court ordered that the case be adjourned until 5 January 2021 and that I, the defendant, would continue to remain in remand.

On 5 January 2021, the case was adjourned again because the state attorney, Mr. Saraji, was on vacation. The magistrate ordered that the case be re-scheduled to 19 January 2021, and that I, the defendant, will remain in custody.

On 19 January 2021, the court session met again for this matter. The prosecutor told the court that the case has come for mention as the hearing will be held on working day. We therefore request that it be postponed. Learned Adv. Faraji Mangula told the court that he was asking for a date to be set as we are now close to the start of the hearing.

The judge adjourned the case and announced that the case would come up for mention after a week towards Law Day. So, the trial is set to begin on 2 February 2021. And I, the defendant, will continue to remain in custody.

On 2 February 2021, before Hon. Z. D Laizer and in the presence of the State Attorney Ms. Tengeneza, the defendant, Clerk Luce, and me, the case came up for mention. The magistrate ordered that the case be heard on 15 and 16 February

2021. He adjourned the case and ordered that the defendant continue to be detained in Ruanda prison.

On 15 February 2021, a court hearing was held before Hon. Z. D. Laizer and attended by State Attorney Mr. Saraji Iboru, I, the defendant, Clerk Luce, but the defense attorney did not appear due to his being sick.

The state's attorney told the court that they had prepared witnesses but the defense attorney was not present. The magistrate ordered the case to be adjourned and that it would come again for hearing on 1 and 2 March 2021. The case then came to court again on March 1, 2021, before Hon. Z. D. Laizer and attended by Mr. Saraji, Mr. Davice, Defense Counsel Adv. Mangula, Clerk Luce, and I, the defendant.

***

The fourth prosecution witness in my case was Semeni Ally Mkina, a fifty-one-year-old woman, a Muslim, a resident of Inyala, and Iyunga entrepreneur working as 'Mama Lishe.' She was sworn in, then led by the state attorney and told the court as follows that she lives in Inyala, and her works are to cook and sell food. She is doing the business in the Forest area near the office of the Regional Police Commander. She has been there for four years.

The State Attorney asked the witness to explain on 12 May 2020 where she was and what happened. The witness explained that on 12 May 2020 she was in her little restaurant. A police officer named Siame came and asked her to accompany him to witness the examination and packaging of samples, which the suspect was found with. The witness went on to say, "He told me that a suspect had been found with objects which are seized by us and are going to send it to a state chemist. I went with him to their offices and found that there were other police officers as well." The witness continued, "It saw five nylon bags with white powder. During the sealing, there were also other officers whom I identified as Chale and Ally, ASP Siame, and the suspect whom I was told that he was called Mdude." The state attorney asked the witness if she had known the accused Mdude before. The witness said she did not know me before. She was again asked if she knew the officers who came for her that day. She replied, "I know them because these officers were my clients at my food booth." The state's attorney asked the witness to explain what happened after she responded to the officers' call. The witness testified that she witnessed the sealing of the envelope and she was left with an officer who took notes. After that, she left.

When asked if she could remember Mdude, she replied, "I don't think I can remember Mdude just by seeing him, maybe if I look for him inside this room." She pointed at me and said, "He is here."

After being led by the state attorney, it was the turn of the Defense Advocate Faraji Mangula to take cross-examine her.

Adv. Mangula: *When you were called to the police station, you found the exhibit already sealed, didn't you?*

Witness Semeni: *I did not find the exhibit sealed.*

Adv. Mangula: *Who was in the office when you entered?*

Witness Semeni: *I found Ally and Chale, who showed me the specimen and started to seal it.*

Adv. Mangula: *You are a small entrepreneur; do you have an entrepreneur's ID as per the requirement of the government?*

Witness Semeni: *I have the ID but in fact, today I did not come with it.*

Adv. Mangula: *How can you prove that you are a food vendor without an ID?*

Witness Semeni: *Since I have not come with it, I have no way to prove that I am safe.*

Adv. Mangula: *When you were called to the police station to witness the sealing of the exhibits, did you put your signature on any form to prove your witness?*

Witness Semen: *I did not sign on any form.*

Adv. Mangula: *Do you know where the exhibit we are talking about is?*

Witness Semeni: *I do not know where it is.*

Adv. Mangula: *Do you know how much that exhibit weighs?*

Witness Semeni: *I do not know or understand anything about the weight of the exhibit. All I know is that the exhibit was in nylon bags.*

Adv. Mangula: *Do you sell food to police officers who work at RPC's office?*

Witness Semeni: *Yes, I do.*

Adv. Mangula: *The officers who asked you to go and witness the sealing of the exhibits, are among the ones you sell food to?*

Witness Semeni: *Yes.*

Adv. Mangula: *Let me know if you know their names.*

Witness Semeni: *ASP Siame, Chale, and Ally himself.*

Adv. Mangula: *Do you agree with me that in your statement you did not tell the court the time you were taken by ASP Siame?*

Witness Semeni: *I did not say yes.*

There, the Defense Counsel, Adv. Mangula had just finished questioning the fourth witness. It was the turn of the state counsel for re-examination.

***

The fifth witness was forty-six-year-old Audifas Pilato Silayo, a resident of Uyole, Christian, and a farmer. He was sworn and testified under the guidance of a state attorney.

The witness told the court that he was a farmer and also the owner of the house that I rented. The witness was asked to explain in court the location of his house. And he answered, "My house is located in Itezi area, Mwasote Street in Mbeya District."

He was asked how many tenants he had rented and whether Mdude was one of his tenants. He replied, "I have fourteen tenants in the house. Mdude is one of my tenants."

The state attorney wanted to know the manager of the house. The witness said it was his younger brother named Peter. He is the one who manages the house and its tenants. He explained that Peter was the one who entered into contract with the tenants and then sent him the tenants' payment. The Witness was asked if he knew Mdude and if he knew when his contract started, he replied, "Peter is the one who knows Mdude and is the one who knows when he rented this house."

The prosecutor asked the witness if he had ever met Mdude. The witness replied that he had never met Mdude before.

When the State Attorney's finished questioning the fifth witness, the Defense Advocate, Mr. Mangula, came in for cross-examining the witness.

Adv. Mangula: *Have you met Mdude before?*
Witness Silayo: *No.*
Adv. Mangula: *Are you the one who signed the contract with Mdude while he was renting the house?*

Witness Silayo: *I did not enter into a tenancy agreement with Mdude.*

Adv. Mangula: *How long do you think Mdude has been in your house?*

Witness Silayo: *I think Mdude has been there for three months.*

Adv. Mangula: *Do you know which political party Mdude is a member of?*

Witness Silayo: *I do not know Mdude's political party.*

Adv. Mangula: *Since Mdude became your tenant, have you ever had any criminal record involving him?*

Witness Silayo: *I have never heard of Mdude having any criminal record.*

The Defense Counsel Adv. Mangula finished questioning the fifth witness and the state attorney came in for re-examination.

***

The sixth witness for the prosecution was CPL Charles, numbered F 4959, D / CPL, a forty-five-year-old man, a resident of the FFU line, Christian in religion, and his job is a police officer. He swore and then under the guidance of a state attorney, told the court that he is a police officer working in the Mbeya RCO office since 2009. The state attorney asked the witness to explain his responsibilities to the RCO office. The witness explained, "My duties include arresting criminals, conducting investigations, and bringing criminals to court."

The witness was required to state in the court where was he and what was he doing on 11 May 2020. The witness explained, "On 11 May 2020, in the afternoon, I was called by RCO

Assistant ASP Siame. When I got to his office, I found him with one person who was introduced to me as lawyer Fadhili Shombe. He told me that we had to go to the central police station to pick up the suspect with the intention of going to his house to conduct a search. I was told that Fadhili is the defendant's lawyer. I went to the central station on a Toyota Land Cruiser. On the way, ASP Siame told me that the suspect was called Mdude and was in custody. When we arrived at the central station, the suspect was released from the remand and his name removed from the suspects' register."

The witness continued, "We started the journey towards Mdude's residence. With me in the caravan were ASP Siame, Mdude himself, lawyer Fadhili and someone else. On the way, when we reached the construction site, Mdude was asked if he had the keys to his house. He replied that he had left them at the central police station. We went back to the station where he was given his keys by the receptionist."

The State Attorney asked the witness how come that the keys remained at the station. The Witness replied, "It is the procedure for the police to take care of the suspect's equipment when he is remanded in custody."

The witness continued, "After that, we headed to Mdude's house in Itezi area, Mwasote Street. When we arrived, we stayed outside waiting for the local leader to come. A neighbor phoned the local leader and he arrived immediately. When the leader arrived, ASP Siame introduced himself to him and that leader introduced himself also. The leader identified himself as a member of ten houses in the area. He was asked if he knew the suspect and he replied yes, he does. The leader was informed that we had gone there with the intention of conducting a search of his local resident's house."

The state's attorney asked the witness to explain if anything had happened before entering the house. The Witness replied, "Before entering Mdude's house, we told him that he had the right to search us before we entered his house. He searched all of us."

The Witness went on to explain, "After searching us, we entered the house. We started a search in his bedroom and then to the living room. Inside the bedroom, we found one phone. We entered another room and found another phone. When we entered the living room, we found on a small table a televisions and CDs. We continued our search on the sofa couches.

During the search, behind the couches on the floor, we found a khaki envelope. We opened it and found a nylon bag. We opened the nylon bag and found five bags of flour. It was suspected that the powder was a drug. Mdude was asked what it was, but he failed to give an explanation."

The witness went on to tell the court that after the search they filled out a special seizure form as per the police force's order. "We filled out a form that we have seized five bags of flour, two phones and several CDs."

The state's attorney asked the witness to explain whether the witnesses present at the search filled out a seizure order. The witness explained, "All those present in the search signed the form." He mentioned that he was accompanied by ASP Siame, a lawyer Fadhili Shombe, the accused himself, and a local leader. He went on, "After that I made a sketch of the scene under the direction of a local leader. After drawing a sketch, the suspect closed his door and we started the journey back to the RCO's office."

The State Attorney asked the witness if he could identify the map he had drawn after the search. He replied that he could identify the map as it had his signature.

The Witness was shown a drawing, and he recognized it as the one he had drawn. The witness asked the court to accept the drawing as an official exhibit.

Attorney Faraji Mangula said he had no objection to the receipt of the exhibit.

The judge ruled that the sketch dated 11 May 2020, would be received and marked as exhibit P13.

The sixth witness went on to tell the court that he could identify the seizure note because he had prepared it and signed it with the person who had previously described it to him. The witness was given a form by the state's attorney and told the court that this was the completed form at the scene. "I prepared it on behalf of ASP Siame and this form was signed by the accused and all the witnesses present at the scene." Regarding a search at Mdude's residence, the witness states that he searched and found nylon bags with powder substance in it… The State Attorney provided the witness with exhibits P5 to P9, and he identified them and told the court that these were the things they had found in the search at Mdude's residence. Holding the exhibit P5, the witness said, "We found this in the suspect's residence, it was locked up as it was and was in powder form. We marked it A1, before we sent it to the state chemist."

The Witness identified all the exhibits in A2, A3, A4, and A5 and explained that they had been found in my residence with a nylon bag inside. "We suspected it was drug."

The state attorney asked the witness to explain what happened next. The Witness went on to explain, "On 12 May 2020, this flour we took from Mdude's residence was marked and sealed and sent to government chemist for investigation in the presence of the accused and witnesses. There was one female citizen who witnessed the sealing event."

The State Attorney asked the witness if he could identify the suspect. The witness told the court that he could identify the suspect and immediately pointed a finger at me, and uttered, "Here he is."

Then the Defense Counsel, Adv. Mangula, stood to begin cross-examining the witness.

Adv. Mangula: *Tell the court about your education.*

Witness Charles: *I have a degree in procurement from TIA Mbeya College, which I received in 2016–2019.*

Adv. Mangula: *With your education, can you read English?*

Witness Charles: *I do not have to know English well, even though I have studied until university.*

Adv. Mangula: *How long have you been a police officer, and how long have you been doing investigative works?*

Witness Charles: *I have been a police officer for twenty-one years and a detective for seventeen years.*

Adv. Mangula: *Do you know what laws guides you in your police and detective activities?*

Witness Charles: *We are led by PGO and I do not know any laws other than PGO.*

Adv. Mangula: *Tell the court what is done to the accused before he is taken into custody.*

Witness Charles: *When the suspect is brought to the detention his properties are confiscated and packed into the PPR and are being stored.*

Adv. Mangula: *Did the procedure described here also apply to Mdude?*

Witness Charles: *When Mdude was brought to the station, I was not there. But I was there when he was released.*

Adv. Mangula: *When he was released, was he given his PPR?*

Witness Charles: *He was not given his PPR as he was expected to be brought back in custody. If he had been released, he would have been given his PPR.*

Adv. Mangula: *When Mdude was returned, was he given his PPR?*

Witness Charles: *Yes. When we returned to the station, Mdude was given his PPR. And he had to hand over his keys.*

Adv. Mangula: *When a suspect is remanded in custody is he allowed leaving his PPR?*

Witness Charles: *No. He hands over to the officer on duty, after which the officer hands over to the suspect.*

Adv. Mangula: *Where is Mdude's PPR?*

Witness Charles: *I do not know where the PPR is.*

Adv. Mangula: *When you were giving your evidence, did you say the keys to Mdude are part of the exhibit?*

Witness Charles: *Yes, I did.*

Adv. Mangula: *Was Mdude's keys listed on PPR?*

Witness Charles: *Yes.*

Adv. Mangula: *How many keys were on the list?*

Witness Charles: *I do not remember the number.*

Adv. Mangula: *When you released Mdude for a search at his residence, did you hand over all his belongings to him?*

Witness Charles: *He was not given his properties as he was expected to be remanded in custody after a search.*

Adv. Mangula: *Where did the search start?*

Witness Charles: *We started a search in Mdude's bedroom.*

Adv. Mangula: *Who were left outside the house?*

Witness Charles: *Our driver and one of the police officers were left outside to guard.*

Adv. Mangula: *If the officers who were outside got into the living room while you were in the bedroom, could you see them?*

Witness Charles: *We could not see them.*

Adv. Mangula: *Tell the court about the bags you claimed to have found.*

Witness Charles: *What we found in those five bags was powder substance.*

Adv. Mangula: *Does the map drawing you brought here in court has a police seal?*

Witness Charles: *This drawing does not have a police force seal. All in all, it is not necessary.*

Adv. Mangula: *Is it a procedure to prepare a sketch of the search scene or is it just your will?*

Witness Charles: *Yes, it is a police procedure.*

Adv. Mangula: *What procedures do you follow when preparing the sketch?*

Witness Charles: *I do not know what the law says, as I have not studied it.*

Adv. Mangula: *Tell the court, what was contained in the CDs you seized from Mdude?*

Witness Charles: *I do not know the allegations against the suspect in the CDs.*

Adv. Mangula: *Do you know which political party Mdude comes from?*

Witness Charles: *I do not know.*

Adv. Mangula: *Which party leads the government?*

Witness Charles: *As far as I know, it is CCM.*

Adv. Mangula: *Which political party competed vigorously against CCM in the general election?*

Witness Charles: *I do not know what the main opposition party is. Many parties contested in the election.*

Adv. Mangula: *In your statement, while led by the state attorney did you explain how Ms. Semeni witnessed the sealing of the exhibits?*

Witness Charles: *I was not questioned on how Semeni witnessed the sealing.*

Adv. Mangula: *Tell the court the name of the government official who witnessed the search.*

Witness Charles: *His name is John.*

Adv. Mangula: *Who signed the seizure form?*

Witness Charles: *The form was signed by the accused himself, a local leader, an assistant to RCO Siame and the lawyer for the accused Fadhili.*

Adv. Mangula: *You did not sign the arrest form?*

Witness Charles: *I did not sign the form.*

Adv. Mangula: *What were the alleged drugs on?*

Witness Charles: *It was in a khaki envelope.*

There the witness was given exhibit P5 to P9. He recognized them and then the questions continued.

Adv. Mangula: *What color are these things in here?*

Witness Charles: *This is white but I am not an expert in color identification.*

Adv. Mangula: *Is the khaki envelope you mentioned here in the court?*

Witness Charles: *The khaki envelope is not here.*

Adv. Mangula: *Where is it?*

Witness Charles: *It was removed while we were doing the sealing.*

Adv. Mangula: *In your statement given here in court, did you state where the Khaki envelope went?*

Witness Charles: *I did not say where the khaki envelope went.*

Adv. Mangula: *Did you conduct a DNA test of the people, who touched the envelope to find out who exactly put the bags containing drugs there?*

Witness Charles: *I am not a geneticist.*

The witness was then given Exhibit P10—which is a seizure note—and the examination continued.

Adv. Mangula: *According to this exhibit, who conducted the search?*

Witness Charles: *The person who conducted the search was myself under the orders of ASP Siame. Although, it is not written under this heading that I was the one who conducted the search, but it is written that ASP Siame was the one who conducted the search.*

The Witness was given Exhibit P13, which is a diagram of the area under investigation. Questions continued.

Adv. Mangula: *In this sketch, where was the alleged envelope containing drugs found?*

Witness Charles: *The envelope was on the floor behind the sofa seat.*

Adv. Mangula: *Is there on this sketch a signature of ASP Siame who led the search?*

Witness Charles: *ASP Siame did not sign the sketch.*

The defense Advocate then completed cross-examination, and then State Attorney stood to take re-examination.

On the same day, the seventh prosecution witness was brought in.

***

The seventh witness for the prosecution was Peter Bwetela, forty-five, a Christian, resident of Uyole, Itezi Gombe North, and a farmer. He was sworn and gave his testimony under the guidance of a State Attorney that; he is a friend of Audifas Silayo who lives in Uyole, in Itezi County. The witness continued, "My friend Silas owns a house that he has given me the responsibility of managing because it has tenants. I often sign a contract with tenants on his behalf. Our contracts are for three months."

The State Attorney asked the witness to explain since when Mdude had been his tenant and if he knew him. The Witness replied, "On 6 July 2019, I received Mr. Mdude Mpaluka Nyagali who wanted to be a tenant in the house. I can recognize him because he was my tenant." The State Attorney asked the witness to show the court where I was. The Witness pointed at me.

The State Attorney asked the witness to explain the agreement and the payment for the house I was living in. The Witness went on saying, "He paid me a total of TSH 300,000 which is a rent of TSH 100,000 per month. After the first three months were over, he sent his brother to pay another TSH 300,000 for another three months. He continued to pay his tenancy bill to me and fill out the contract form as required. I can recognize contracts because it has my signature."

The Witness was given a document by the State Attorney, and he recognized it as an agreement between him and Mdude. He asked the court to accept the document as an exhibit.

Defense lawyer Faraji Mangula objected to the acceptance of the document in the court on the grounds that it did not contain a government tax stamp. Pursuant to Stamp Duty Act No. 20 of 1972, Section 46 (1), only the taxable document can be received as proof of evidence before the law. Contracts must have a tax stamp for the government to recover its revenue as required by the law. "I am against the receipt of this document because it shows that they have evaded taxes," said Adv. Mangula.

The State Attorney responded by saying that the bringing of this objection was unfounded. That the government is not getting its tax does not make the contract worthless and enforceable. "Our answer is no. The contract can be verbal or written. The government has a way of getting its revenue from buildings. The objection should be on whether the client is aware of the contract or not. Since the objection is only on taxation, we now request that both agreements be accepted as exhibit," said the State Attorney.

State Attorney Mr. Davice clarified that the witness who brings the exhibits is the one who made and signed them, so he has the right to present them in court.

Defense Advocate Mangula then told the court that his fellow State Attorneys agreed that the contracts did not have a tax stamp. "These are the contracts set out in the text; they must have a tax stamp. The only way the government can get its tax return is by putting a tax stamp on it. We therefore request that these tenancy agreements not be accepted as an exhibit here in court."

As a result of these discussions, the court ruled that the objection was fundamental, but the deficiencies in these documents could be remedied. The magistrate said, "The law requires contracts like this be stamped with a tax stamp so that it can be a legal representation. I therefore order that these contracts be taxed and then be brought to court as an exhibit."

The State Attorney then asked the court to adjourn for ten minutes so that they could stamp the contracts. The magistrate gave them ten minutes for the task. After ten minutes, the prosecution came back with contracts with tax stamps. Advocate Mangula said he had no objection to the acceptance of the contracts in court.

The court ruled that the contracts dated 6 July 2019 and 1 April 2020 were received in court and marked P14 together.

Witness 7 continued by reading exhibit P14 together, one after another, "The contract is for three months. After Mdude was arrested and detained, his brother Masonga came and paid rent for another three months. After three months, he came and asked me to remove Mdude's belongings as he felt he could not bear the cost of continuing to pay for the house." When the State Artorney asked the witness if he had received reports of Mdude's arrest, the witness said he was told by a member of the ten houses and Mr. Masonga that Mdude was arrested in November 2020.

Witness Peter went on to explain, "Mdude was my very good tenant. He lived well in my house. He had good relations with his fellow tenants. I have never received any complaints against him from his fellow tenants."

After chief examination from the State Attorney, it was then the turn of Defense Advocate Mangula to start cross-examining the witness.

Adv. Mangula: *Are you the owner of the house where Mdude lives?*

Witness Peter: *I am not the owner of the house but only the manager.*

Adv. Mangula: *Have you ever heard of any criminal news about Mdude?*

Witness Peter: *I have never heard of Mdude having any criminal record.*

Adv. Mangula: *Have you ever had any argument with Mdude?*

Witness Peter: *I personally never argued with Mdude and did not evict him from the house.*

After the testimony from the seventh witness, the State Attorney asked the court to adjourn the case until the following day. The magistrate ordered that the court be adjourned until tomorrow, 2 March 2021, at ten o'clock in the morning. And I, the suspect, will continue to be remanded in Ruanda prison.

***

On 2 March 2021, the court continued under Hon. Z. D. Laizer and attended by State Attorney Mr. Saraji Iboru, Defense Counsel Mr. Faraji Mangula and I, the accused myself. The clerk of the court was Luce. The State Attorney said the case had come for a hearing, and Advocate Faraji Mangula said that the defense side is ready to proceed.

Witness continued to be given by the eighth witness. This was Mr. John Rasek Manyumba, a fifty-one-year-old man, a resident of Itezi, Mwasita. His works as a farmer and his is Christian in religion. The witness swore and began to give his testimony as led by the State Attorney, "In Mwasita Street, I am a member of ten houses cell number 10. I have been a leader there since 2017. My job is to keep the peace and protect my people as well as to resolve minor disputes in my area."

The State Attorney asked witness John to explain before the court on what happened on 11 May 2020. The Witness went on to tell the court that on that day, at one p.m., he was in the market. He was phoned by a man who introduced himself as ACP Charles from police headquarters. "He called me in my area as there was a problem needing my urgent response. After receiving the instructions, I hired a bicycle and rushed to the scene. I found police officers and a suspect whom I identified as Mdude. They asked me if I knew the suspect, and I replied that I knew him by the name of Mdude because he is my neighbor in here. But as a leader, I do not know him well, as when he moved to this place, he did not come with a letter to introduce himself to me."

The State Attorney asked the witness to say as to whether the police officers at the scene were in or outside the house. The witness said they were outside the house because the house was fenced. He went on to explain, "They told me they wanted to search the house where Mdude lives. Mdude opened the door, and we went inside."

The State Attorney asked the witness to explain whether Mdude had been given the opportunity to conduct a search on all of those available searchers as required by law. The witness said, "Mdude did a search for us as required by law in a situation like this."

The Witness went on to give his statement, "After that, we went into the house where he lives. This is a house with two bedrooms, living room, and toilet. After we entered, Mdude closed the door from inside. The search started in the bedroom.

Police found one small Samsung phone. He entered to another room and continued his search, where he found Nokia phone. They searched the toilet but found nothing. We came to the living room and did a search where they found khaki envelope on the floor under the sofa coach. They opened it and found nylon bags. They were wrapped in small bundles of flour. They also found about twenty-four CDs, which they also took. After taking all those items, they opened their notebook and we all had to sign. They ordered me to accompany them to the main police station so that I could sign their forms there. I accompanied them to the station, where I wrote down my report on the incident."

When asked if he could identify the seizure note, they had obtained after conducting a search, the witness told the court that the document was signed by him, Mdude, and a police officer. He said he could identify the document because it contained his handwriting, his name, and his signature. The witness was given exhibit number P10, identified it and stated that the document was correct. "It has a list of items found inside the house. It also has my name and signature, the signatures of the lawyer Fadhili Shombe and of the accused."

The witness said he could identify the five specimens that were wrapped in nylon bags. "Its color was yellow. If I am shown I will be able to identify them." The Witness was given exhibits from P5 to P9; he identified them, and said that these were the items they found in the house. "Yes, these are the items we seized. The color is the same. And they were five in total." The witness was asked to identify me in the court he pointed at me and said, "Mdude is here in court."

After the examination was done from the witness by State Attorney the Defense Counsel, Advocate Mangula stood to cross-examine the eighth witness.

Adv. Mangula: *Please tell the court about your education.*

Witness John: *I only went to school up to standard seven of primary school.*

Adv. Mangula: *Do you have ability to speak Kiswahili and English fluently?*

Witness John: *I can speak Swahili well but I can't speak any English word.*

Adv. Mangula: *You said you are a farmer. When you were led by a state attorney, did you tell what kind of produce you cultivate?*

Witness John: *The Attorney did not question me about the type of produce I cultivate.*

Adv. Mangula: *Did you tell the lawyer how you got the local leadership?*

Witness John: *He also did not ask me how I got the leadership in the area.*

Adv. Mangula: *Show the court your leadership ID.*

Witness John: *I did not come with my leadership ID.*

Adv. Mangula: *Do you know what charges Mdude has been brought to court for?*

Witness John: *I do not know what charges the accused has in this court.*

Adv. Mangula: *What law requires a person to write a letter of introduction to a leader when he or she moves to another house?*

Witness John: *I do not know.*

Adv. Mangula: *Since Mdude moved to your street has he ever been charged with any criminal offense?*

Witness John: *This suspect has never been suspected in any crime.*

Adv. Mangula: *Have you told the State Attorney how Mdude closed the door?*

Witness John: *I did not say anywhere how Mdude closed the door.*

Adv. Mangula: *While searching the Mdude's bedroom, can you see someone coming into the living room from the outside?*

Witness John: *From the bedroom, we could see who was going into the living room.*

Adv. Mangula: *If another witness says you can't see the living room from the bedroom, contrary to what you have just said, whom should the court believe?*

Witness John: *The court will decide whom to trust if there is a dispute.*

Adv. Mangula: *In your statement you said, the CDs were found in the room, if another witness appeared and say the CDs were found in the living room, whom should the court believe?*

Witness John: *The court will decide whom to trust.*

Adv. Mangula: *You said the powder found in the suspect's home was yellow in color. If another witness appeared and say they were white, whom will the court believe?*

Witness John: *The court itself will decide whom to trust.*

The witness was then given an exhibit P10 and told to read. He read it all, and then continued to be questioned.

Adv. Mangula: *What is this?*

Witness John: *This is a khaki envelope.*

Adv. Mangula: *Are you sure?*

Witness John: *I'm not sure if it looks the same, as it was the day we seized it.*

Adv. Mangula: *What is this?* (Showing the powder bags)

Witness John: *That's what we found that day.*

Adv. Mangula: *What color were they the day you seized them?*

Witness John: *They had this same color.*

Adv. Mangula: *Local government elections were held in 2019, when were you elected?*

Witness John: *I was elected in 2017 and my term ends in 2022.*

Adv. Mangula: *Who was holding the suspect's keys when you reached his home?*

Witness John: *The defendant himself had his keys.*

The witness was subsequently corrected by the state's attorney, after which the state attorney asked the court to close the evidence. The court closed the indictment.

V
MY DEFENSE

"True democracy is the one built on the foundations of good constitution, clean policies, free people and free institutions."
– Mdude M. Nyagali

Based on the evidences presented in the court by the prosecution, the magistrate Z. D. Laizer handed down the minor verdict and informed me that the court had found that I have a case to answer. In that sense, I had to produce my defense in relation to the allegations against me.

My lawyer, Advocate Faraji Mangula, told the court that I, the accused, would present my defense under oath and there would be two witnesses and four exhibits. "I am asking you to register a document to add witnesses and exhibits for the sole purpose of making justice prevail. Thank you very much," said Advocate Mangula.

Adv. Mangula then asked the court to set another date for the mention of the case as he has health problems. The court ordered that the case be mentioned on 16 March 2021 and heard on 25 March 2021.

On 16 March 2021, the case was brought before Hon. Z. D. Laizer and attended by state attorney Mr. Tengeneza, Clerk Luce, and I, the defendant, participated via the internet while incarcerated. The State Attorney told the court that the case had come up for mention and that it would come up for a hearing on 25 March 2021.

On 25 March 2021, the court continued before Hon. Z. D. Laizer and attended by State Attorneys Mr. Saraji and Mr. Davice, and I, the defendant myself, was present along with my lawyer, Advocate Faraji Mangula. The Clerk of the Court was Luce.

The State Attorney said they were ready, and Advocate Mangula said we are ready, and today they have two witnesses. The first defense witness (DW1) was myself, Mdude Mpaluka Nyagali, a thirty-two-year-old resident of Itezi, Uyole. My religion is Christian and my occupation is a politician. I was sworn in and began to testify, as led by Adv. Faraji Mangula.

Mr. Mangula wanted me to tell the court who am I in the community and what my daily responsibilities are. I informed the court that I am the leader working with CHADEMA, a political party, as a training officer in the Nyasa zone, which includes the regions of Iringa, Njombe, Mbeya, Rukwa, and Songwe. I am also an activist for Human Rights and Good Governance. Adv. Mangula wanted me to tell the court what CHADEMA is. I replied that CHADEMA is an acronym for the *Chama cha Demokrasia na Maendeleo*. It is a political party registered here in Tanzania.

Advocate Mangula wanted me to tell the court as to when I started human rights movements and the challenges I went through. I replied that I have been an activist since 2009. So, I have more than ten years in the movement. In my political activities, I have experienced many and very great tragedies, and I have also witnessed other people suffer a lot. I have witnessed police officers breaking the law and violating human rights by torturing people and convicting suspects illegally. Police officers have been making false accusations and prosecuting people. I have said this from time to time through social media and public meetings. They unlawfully arrest people, kill innocent civilians, and impose fear among the society. I longed to remind them that they are not above the law. I myself have been arrested and given false charges, and later the court acquits me because the police officers always fail to prove allegations against me.

I went on to tell the court that on 26 August 2016, I was arrested by a police officer at my home in Ichenjezya, Songwe region. Police officers arrested me without any legal restraint, and they never told me what I had done. Furthermore, they searched my house and confiscated some of my belongings without even a search warrant or an independent witness. They detained and tortured me for seventeen days against the laws of the land and. On 13 September 2016, they took me to court on charges of sedition. But I was acquitted of the charge for lack of complete evidence.

Advocate Mangula asked me what I had done after being released by the court. I replied that after my release, I wrote a letter to the Commission for Human Rights and Good Governance. The reason I wrote the letter was because I thought of other people who have been tortured by the police force. I saw that my torment would save many people from being arrested and tortured by the police illegally. In the letter, I explained how the police had arrested me and confiscated my personal belongings. I also described how I was ridiculed and persecuted. I explained how I had been transported to Dar es Salaam and locked up in a concentration camp for seventeen days. I was not taken to court within a reasonable time as stated by the law.

Advocate Faraji Mangula wanted me to tell the court if there were any other incidents that plagued me in the process of defending Human Rights and good governance. I continued to inform the court about other cases of torture by the police force. That on 4 May 2019, at six p.m., I was abducted by people who identified themselves as policemen.

The incident took place about 200 meters from the Songwe regional police headquarters. I asked my captors to show me their IDs if they were really police officers and also from which police station they were from, following my procedural request to them before the arrest, they became so furious, and the violence erupted. They were fully armed and had two cars.

I screamed for help, but the kidnappers fired loudly to disperse the people who came to help me. They managed to grab me and was thrown in one of the cars. They then started punching me on various parts of my body, especially on my head. I was severely beaten until I fainted.

On 8 May 2019, I was picked up by good Samaritans in Inyala village in Mbeya region. The people who picked me up took me to the village chairman, and called the police but they did not show up. That's when he called CHADEMA leaders. Officials came to pick me up and took me to the Mbeya Regional Referral Hospital. That same night, my relatives went to the police station to ask for PF3 for medical treatment but the police refused to issue it.

I went on by telling the court that even when my relatives went to report that I had been abducted, the police refused to open a file for investigation. When MP Peter Msigwa presented the matter to the parliament and to the Minister of Home Affairs, the Deputy Minister of Home Affairs Hon. Hamad Masauni ordered before parliament that the file should be opened immediately. However, to date no one has been arrested in connection with my abduction and torture. After that incident, the following month, in May, I filed a notice to sue the police force for the atrocities they had inflicted on me, including the 2016 torture as well as holding me for twenty-one days illegally in 2017.

Advocate Faraji Mangula then asked if I could remember the letter, I wrote to the Human Rights and Good Governance Commission. I replied that I could recognize the letter because it contained my name and signature. I also remember what I wrote in it. Adv. Mangula handed me the letter and I looked at it. I proved it was the same. Adv. Mangula went on to ask me if I would like the letter to be received as an exhibit in my case in this court. I asked the court to accept this letter as an exhibit to show how bad my relations with the police are.

State Attorney Mr. Saraji objected for the letter to be received as an exhibit on the grounds that it was not a letter sent to the Human Rights Commission. He said that since I had sent the letter by e-mail, then I had to bring an e-mail to the court. His other argument was that this letter had handwriting and drawings on the back and nothing was said about that handwriting. "There is no indication that this letter was sent to the commission. Since it was sent by email then we request the same electronic mail be brought. That's all," said State Attorney, Saraji.

Defense Counsel Adv. Faraji Mangula responded by saying that the witness had stated that he had written the letter and had signed it. "According to the law of evidence, it is the only real document that is recognized as an exhibit in giving evidence. The Exhibit is up to the address to which this letter was sent. We, therefore request that this letter be received as an exhibit under rule 64 (1) of the evidence law."

Advocate Faraji went on saying, "The State Attorney has not indicated which law prohibits the receipt of such an actual letter. Some text is on the back of the letter. We target the location of the typewriter letter. I, therefore, request the court to accept this letter as an exhibit."

The state's attorney insisted that the witness had stated that he had sent a letter by email. So, in order to get the accuracy of this exhibit then he has to bring the letter he sent by email. And it must have been printed from the website he used to send the letter.

After the dispute between the two lawyers, the court ruled that the objection lodged by the state attorney was not valid, as the witness had told the court that he had written a letter to the Commission. Objection is thrown away. Therefore, my letter dated 3 May 2017, sent to the Human Rights and Good Governance Commission was received as an exhibit D1, and based on the handwriting on the back of some of the pages of the letter, it can be used for clarification during the examinations in this court.

When the court agreed to receive the letter, I told her that the handwritten note had nothing to do with the message in the letter. This handwriting I wrote while I was incarcerated during my interrogation by my lawyer Martin. I did not have any paper to write on in the custody so I had to use the back of the letter. It is a letter I wrote myself on my computer, and then I printed this letter to sign.

The people at the Commission for Human Rights and Good Governance wrote to the Inspector General Police (IGP) informing him of my complaint. A copy was sent to me and they wanted me to send a copy of the judgment of the case I won. I received the letter via email.

I continued by saying that I issued to the police force a ninety-day notice of intention to sue them for tortures and humiliations they had inflicted on me. After those ninety days, I filed a case in the Mbeya High Court. In that case, I, Mdude Nyagali, sued the Attorney General, the IGP, the Songwe Regional Police Commander (RPC), and several police officers. I have a copy of the documents for that case. The case is for litigation No. 1/2019, which was heard by Hon. Judge Adam Mambi. Here we have one copy of the documents for the case. The original document was lost in custody while prison guards conducted search inside the prison.

Adv. Mangula asked me if I could identify the case documents. I replied that I could identify the case documents as they contained my name and the names of those I had sued. Advocate Faraji handed me the documents and asked me if they were genuine, and I replied that they were the same and the documents I used to file the case on 28 August 2019 in the High Court at Mbeya. After identifying them, Adv. Mangula asked me if I would like the documents to be provided as an exhibit. I replied that I requested these documents be received as an exhibit. This document contains an appendix that is one of the judgments of my cases.

Advocate Faraji Mangula asked the court to accept the copies and that the court should recognize them as original documents. "Section 67 (1) (c) of the Evidence Act chapter 6 of 2019 allows for the receipt of a copy of the original documents. Similarly, this document is public in accordance with rule 83 (a) (ii). The court that heard this case is the High Court, so I request that this exhibit be received in court in accordance with rule 59 (1) of the evidence / exhibition law by notice. Judicial," said Adv. Mangula.

The State Attorney did not object to the receipt of the documents, and the court received indictment in case number 1/2019 as exhibit D2.

Adv. Mangula asked me what my intentions in the indictment in Exhibit D2 were. I replied that the purpose of the charges against the police was to remind them of their responsibility to respect the law. They should not do things, which are not allowed by the laws of the land. They are not above the law. I also aimed to show them that they can be prosecuted but also to help other people who are victims of police force's persecutions.

The appendix to this document is a judgment in criminal case no. 128/2016 heard by Hon. Chami in Mbozi District Court. There is also an attachment, which is a notice, as well as a copy of the letter from the Commission for Human Rights and Good Governance written to the IGP to inform him of my complaint. Adv. Mangula asked me if I could identify the letter, and I informed him that I could identify it as it is from the Commission for Human Rights and Good Governance to the IGP, and I was given a copy from the real letter. Adv. Faraji Mangula wanted me to state my address to which the letter was sent. I replied that my email address to which the letter was sent was *mdudenyagali@gmail.com*. Adv. Mangula handed me the letter and asked if it was the same. I recognized it and told the court that this was a copy of a letter from the Commission on Human Rights and Good Governance to the IGP, which I was also given a copy. Adv. Mangula asked me if I would like the letter to be received as an exhibit in the ongoing court case against me. I replied, "Yes, I ask the court to accept it as an exhibit."

The learned advocate Mangula told the court that they are asking for the letter to be received under section 67 (1) (d) of the exhibition law, "A real letter cannot be easily obtained from the Commission on Human Rights and Good Governance. It was also impossible to certify it as he did not have the original letter."

The state attorney said he had no objection. The court received a copy of the letter dated 4 May 2017 to be received as Exhibit and was marked D3.

Adv. Mangula asked me to explain to the court whether there was any connection between the case I filed against the police which was being heard by the High Court at Mbeya and my charges of drug trafficking. I went on to tell the court that after having filed the case I began to receive threats from police force. I was called and told to drop the case in court otherwise; I would suffer more than I did before. I was not threatened at all because it is not my culture to fear threats from rulers.

On 5 May 2020, the case was scheduled to be heard in which I would begin to testify. The respondents did not appear in court. The judge ordered that the case would be heard on 1 and 2 June 2020 and ordered the respondents to appear in court on the scheduled dates.

On 9 May 2020, I received a call from a person I know by the name of XB and a fellow CHADEMA member, informing me that there was a police officer from the RCO Mbeya office who needed my phone number. He chose to call me before handing the number to him. He explained that the officer had asked him where I could be at that time.

I allowed him to give him my number and that I am very much available at the CHADEMA party offices located in Kadege Mbeya. And if that officer needs me, he will find me there. He told me that he gave him my numbers. But I did not receive any call from the police that day.

On 10 May 2020, I was at home cleaning my house and washing my clothes. Having completed those jobs at home, I left and headed to the office. While in the office continuing with my day-to-day responsibilities, The Songwe Regional Secretary for

CHADEMA Mr. Fadhili Shombe brought in forms for parliamentary and council aspirants. It should be remembered that we were heading to the 2020 General Election.

After Shombe handed me the forms I sent a statement to the party headquarters for further instructions. A few minutes past six o'clock in the evening, I closed the office. As we were leaving, Shombe and I, each of us heading for his home, we were shocked to see four people around me. They introduced themselves as police officers. They told me that they needed me for further interrogations. I asked them; you are dressed in civilian clothes and even using a car with civilian numbers. How do I know as to whether you are real police officers?

One of them issued an ID and introduced himself as ASP Siame and works in the RCO Mbeya office. I asked him what crime has I committed to worth me be arrested to the police custody. He replied that the RCO had ordered my arrest. I told the *bodaboda* people who had parked their motorcycles out there that if I will not be seen again then let them know that the responsible persons are these police officers under ASP Siame. I also told ASP Siame that since you only want my information then my witness would be my friend Shombe. One of them suggested that I be searched. They took my phone, the keys to my house and the keys to the CHADEMA offices, and Shombe's phone. We were boarded into police force's Land Cruiser Hardtop.

We were taken to the RCO office building and taken into one of their offices. One of the police officers started chasing Shombe by kicking him and telling him, "Get out from here, you have ruined our mission." They dragged him out until they tore his jacket. From outside, he asked for his phone, which was finally given to him through the window. I asked them to hand Shombe the keys to my office and my house but they answered with a loud voice, "Shut up." Fadhili Shombe was forcibly removed, and I was left alone in their midst. Afterwards, the Mbeya Regional Criminal Investigation Officer, RCO Katimbo, stepped in. My captors asked me if I knew him. I replied that I know him because he is the one who represents the Inspector General of Police (IGP) in the case I filed against the police. They told me that they wanted to interview me about my family, if I had a wife. That question was asked by Katimbo. They asked me if I was paid by Europeans. Another was writing, but it was not an official interview. They perused through my phone to see if there was money. They questioned me about case number 1 of 2019 that I filed against them. They asked me what gives me the courage to file the case against the police force. RCO Katimbo said that I had gone beyond the limit by suing the IGP and that the IGP is the one who have made me reach this high. I will not tolerate your deeds to him and the force. In his remarks, RCO Katimbo said he had been lifted by the IGP, meaning he had been carried too far to reach his position. That is to say, the RCO meant he did not reach that position by his own ability but by the favors of the IGP. However, in this tragedy, RCO Katimbo has disguised himself as a defender of the IGP. What I did not know is as to whether he was sent by the IGP or himself.

I asked RCO Katimbo, "What is the reason for my arrest?" He did not give me an answer. They ordered me to get off the chair and sit on the floor. I obeyed and descended to the floor. They told me I had a case of incitement. I asked them, "What specifically have I done?" They told me there were words I had posted on Twitter that aimed at creating hatred against President Magufuli and his government. I told them, "Then let me write my details about these allegations." They did not accept it but kept checking the names on my phone. Eventually, they took me to the information room where we found Inspector Joram. He introduced himself to me and told me that I was involved in cybercrime and that I had posted provocative information about President Magufuli on social media.

I asked Inspector Joram to show me the post. However, he did not show me the post and on instead he told me that he is following it up. Here, I found out why the charges against me were not ready and why they had chased Shombe. What is their plan against me? While we were in the first room, one of them, who was wearing a mask, asked me if I remembered him. Before answering, I wondered why he was asking me if I remembered him. Considering I had been abducted by people who introduced themselves as police officers, it was necessary for me to be extra careful when answering such questions. I replied, "I do not remember him." He then unmasked himself and later I remembered that he was among those abducted me in May 2019. After a while, Inspector Joram was called out of the interview room and left me alone. He soon returned and told me that he was taking me to a central police station and that information would be taken on the next day.

After giving this information, Adv. Mangula wanted me to tell the court when I was arrested what did the officers take from me. I replied that when I was arrested, I was robbed of my phone and keys, and they are yet to be returned to me. I showed them the phone I was using on social media, but they insisted on holding all my phones and keys as well. Adv. Mangula asked me at what time was taken to the central police station and to explain if, before I was remanded in custody, there were properties, I registered thereat which I have said was confiscated by the police. I went on to tell the court that we left the RCO office building and headed for the central station. It was between seven to eight o'clock in the evening. I had nothing, and so when I got to the station, I told them that I did not have any property, so I could not be given PPR. They locked me in custody, and I slept there.

On 11 May 2020, Shombe arrived at the station accompanied by police officers. He informed me that the General Secretary of my party, CHADEMA, had instructed him to inquire for the reasons of my arrest. The Secretary General wanted to know what the charges were so that he could send lawyers from Dar es Salaam to deal with my case. He told me that they refused him to see me until he had to apply for a permit from the RCO himself. They told Shombe that they wanted to search my house before they told him what my charges were.

I went on to inform the court that I was taken along with six others heading to my residence for what they said was to conduct search in there. Shombe had come with my brother Michael Mwamlima. Of those seven, civilians, we were three and the rest were police officers led by ASP Siame. When we arrived at the Mafiati area, an officer who came to testify here and whose name I unfortunately do not remember asked ASP Siame if he had the keys for my house. Siame asked, "What keys?" The officer answered him, "Mdude's keys." Siame fumbled and found himself without those keys and that he had forgotten them in the office. ASP Siame then ordered the car to turn around and return to pick the keys from the RCO's office and not the Central Police Station. When we got to their office, the officer who asked about the keys got off and went into the office to bring the keys for house and then came back to the car.

I continued to testify that when he returned, he showed me the keys, got into the car, and we started the journey. When we got to my house, we found another police car with several police officers with firearms. Adv. Mangula asked me as to why I left Vwawa in Songwe region and moved to Mbeya city. I replied that I had moved to these urban areas so that I could be closer to medical services after experiencing severe head and foot problems caused by torture from officers of state agencies. But the persecutors still wanted to torture me, as if tortures were their primary responsibility.

I went on to tell the court that the soldiers in the two vehicles were communicating over the phone all the time before we got home. When we arrived, we all got out of the car. I went inside the fence of my house. Our homes are isolated. I showed the police the house I was living in.

They told me they wanted to call a leader of the ten houses before starting the search. I rejected that and told them that the one who deserved to be a free witness in the search was the local chairman or his executive officer. These are the ones who are elected and have the seal of the government. Even when I moved here, I sent a letter of introduction to them. These are also the ones who witnessed me entering into a rental agreement with the landlord. I told them that the member of the ten houses is the CCM leader at the grassroots level. According to the laws of the land, the leadership of the state begins in the street and in the rural areas in the village. Now the envoy introduced himself here in court as a member of the cell. The government has no leadership in the cell and instead the trunk is the lowest leadership of the CCM. And if you want to call him then call members of other parties as well. But they replied that I should not teach them to work.

I went on to inform the court that from my home to the office of the chairman and local executive is about 300 meters. But we waited for more than half an hour when they came in with a member of ten CCM houses. Before the CCM leader of ten houses came, the tall police officer with the keys, who also came to testify, handed me the keys. I opened the lock, and he told me to wait until the CCM's cell leader to come. I would like it to be known that I was handed the keys to my house after arriving home.

When this CCM leader arrived, they asked me if I knew him, and I replied I did not know him. He introduced himself to me. I insisted that this was not a government official. I explained that government officials start at the local level and there is a chairman and his elected members as well as a local executive. After local leadership in the village or street, we get to ward, district, regional and national leadership. I continued to insist that the cell leaders are partisan and not the government. The one you brought is from CCM and that is why I do not know him. I also told them that CHADEMA leaders are starting from the grassroots. So, if you want this then the leaders of all the parties at the grassroots level and foundation should be brought here. But they continued to despise me.

They forced me to open the door. ASP Siame introduced the officers who will be participating in the search operation at my home. I searched three of the officers, ASP Siame being one of them. They told me to open the door and leave it open. I did so and opened the curtains as well. As soon as we entered the living room, which is the first room to enter, I asked them to show me or even the CCM leader, a search warrant but they did not show it. ASP Siame ordered that the search should begin in my bedroom. I told him that if we did that, we would close the living room door so that no one would come in and put things while we were in the bedroom. Siame refused.

I went on to inform the court that when you enter the house I live in, you first get in the living room. Then there is the veranda separating the living room from the bedrooms. I told them I'm not comfortable to leave police officers in the living room and others outside my house while we search the bedroom. But ASP Siame refused to close the door, stating that the officers who were in the living room and outside were there for security purpose. But the truth is this that they were free to move in and out and do anything without my knowledge.

When I wanted to search them, ASP Siame refused and forced me to go to my bedroom so that the search could begin. They started a search. The tall officer opened the door and went out. I did not know the motive of that. When he returned, I asked him where he had gone, and he replied that I had searched him in the beginning so I don't have to doubt him.

I kept telling the court that the tall officer came out again and after about five minutes, he came back holding gloves. He said he went to the car to pick up the gloves. When I asked him how he got in without being searched again he ignored my argument and continued the search. After searching my room, we moved to search the closet. After searching there, we went into another room and did a search as well. In the guest room, they found my brother's phone and bag. They picked up the phone and searched his bag. Finally, we entered the living room to continue the search. We went to the TV set table where they took my CDs. Then they went to the sofa. They searched but did not find anything. They informed me that the search was over and handed out a form to fill in, the captured specimens and begin to fill it out.

ASP Siame came out and joined the other officers, after about two minutes he returned and told the tall officer that he was worried the search in the living room had not been done properly. He ordered the officer to search under the sofa. As he searched under the sofa, he saw a khaki envelope. He told his colleagues to give him gloves to wear before holding the envelope.

It should be noted that the search started in the bedroom and there were various envelopes with my documents but they held them without wearing gloves except for this envelope found under the sofa they used gloves before seizing it. I wondered in my mind; why did some of the envelopes were held without wearing gloves? The answer I got after asking myself these questions was that these police officers knew what was inside the envelope before holding it.

He took the envelope and asked me, "What is this?" Before I could answer, he replied to himself, "These are drugs." I asked them to show me the drugs so that I could be satisfied with their claim but they refused to show me on the pretext that they would show me the evidence. I was not at all satisfied with the search. However, my two brothers and a leader of ten CCM houses were taken back to the police station.

After this explanation, Adv. Mangula gave me Exhibit P4 which is a nylon bag carrying five small bags containing samples that are alleged to be drugs. Adv. Mangula then asked me about the nylon bag if it was the one found in my home. I said no because in my house they found a khaki envelope with nothing written on it and not this nylon bag. I told the court that the khaki envelope found in my home was not in court. However, I did not see what was inside the envelope. When they seized the envelope, they said it contained drugs; I wanted a genetic test to be conducted because the police officer had seized it while wearing gloves. In that way, we would know exactly who has held the envelope before. I had just cleaned my house just a day ago. I did not see anything like it. So, when they found the envelope, I was very much surprised. To make matters worse, they did not show me what was in the envelope. It was necessary for the envelope to be brought to court for fingerprint tests between me and the officers who were searching my house to determine who had held the envelope before. But the prosecution failed to deliver the envelope.

After explaining that, the Adv. Mangula gave me an exhibit number P10, which was a document to seize the suspect's properties. He then asked me to tell the court why I signed the document when I was not satisfied with the search. I replied that there were other items seized and are enlisted on this form. I signed it as there were items confiscated by the officers including a phone and CDs. So, I asked ASP Siame to give me a form to fill in the shortfalls that had arisen in the search but Siame told me that I would write my details at the police. So, I signed it.

Adv. Mangula asked me to tell the court what matters I was not satisfied with during the search. I went on to inform the court that the first thing I was not satisfied with was the way my keys were kept in custody. The keys were not in the PPR but were in the office for the RCO as it came to light after Siame forgot them and we went back to follow them. When they first arrested me, I asked them to hand over the keys to Shombe but they refused. The second thing I wanted to complain about was that the independent witness from my neighborhood who came to witness the search was not a government official but a CCM member while I was a CHADEMA leader. This is illegal. Thirdly, I wanted to complain about the act of starting a search from my bedroom and leaving the living room's door open, while other unidentified police officers were outside. This made it easier for them to put anything in my living room because when you were in the bedroom you could not see anyone coming into the living room. I was also not given any other form to sign at my residence other than the seizure form. Also, the contents of the khaki envelope were neither shown nor initially examined to determine if it was indeed a drug.

Adv. Mangula gave me Exhibit P13, which is a sketch map of my house. He then asked me to explain the features in the sketch. I explained that in this diagram represents veranda where the police officers who were not searching stood. They told me that they were standing there for security purposes. The search started at area E. There is a door leading to the corridor to the end of the living room. The diagram does not show the toilet that we have searched and it is in front of room E. With this diagram when we went to search room E, we went to room F after which we came to the living room. During the search, the door to the living room was wide open. The door to the corridor leading to the rooms was not shown in the diagram.

Adv. Mangula gave me the exhibit P11, and then asked me to tell the court if the weight of the samples was weighed at my residence as shown in exhibit P11. I went on to tell the court that this exhibit was not tested at my residence. Adv. Mangula handed me the indictment stating that the sample contained drugs weighing 23.4 grams; the exhibit itself reads 23 grams. There is a difference in the weight of those samples recorded in the indictment and exhibit P11. But also Advocate Mangula wanted me to see if there was any place the indictment showed I was transporting these drugs from where to where. I replied that the document does not show and that the indictment does not contain an estimate of the value of the drugs.

I continued to provide my testimony that the document does not indicate whom I was sending these drugs to or to whom I was selling them. I have never smuggled or used drugs. If they suspect that I am using drugs, how difficult was it for them to undertake drug test on me? Also, I have never traveled abroad.

Adv. Mangula gave me exhibit number P12. He then proceeded to ask me if in this exhibit there is anywhere written the weight of those samples and also if there is a part that the exhibit shows the drugs as they were found in my residence. I replied that there was no indication that the allegations were true.

I went on to tell the court that I was aware of these drug charges when I was brought before the court. I demanded to write a statement about how the whole search was flawed, but they refused. No police officer agreed to take my independent information. I have never been involved in any drug trade. There is no evidence that I have been smuggling drugs. It shows that they have made a case for me due to the existence of a very bad relationship between them and me. I have never used drugs, and I do not why they were not ready to go for a DNA test on the khaki envelope they picked up at my house.

Advocate Mangula gave me exhibit number D1, which is a letter I wrote to the Commission on Human Rights and Good Governance. Then he asked me to read the title of the letter, 'REQUEST TO THE COMMISSION.' And I read. After reading it, the Adv. Mangula wanted me to explain how I know Ben Saanane, who was among the people I asked the commission to investigate his disappearance.

And I went on to explain that Ben Saanane was a fellow officer within Chama cha Demokrasia na Maendeleo (CHADEMA). He and I were in constant contact with each other. Ben brought me food while I was being held at the Oysterbay Police Station. He went missing in late 2016. A report was released to the police, but to date, he has not been found.

Adv. Mangula told the court that was all we had for today. After the Advocate Faraji Mangula concluded, the State Attorney Mr. Davice told the court, that it is now 5.46 p.m., we ask for another day to continue with hearing. The plea was not accepted by the defense and counsel Advocate Mangula. He objected to the request, reminding that the case had taken too long, and that the prosecution had two lawyers so it was possible to proceed that day. "It is expensive for me to travel from Dar es Salaam to come here" he conveyed Advocate Mangula.

State attorney Saraji defended his argument by saying that they had many questions that could take two hours or more to discuss. "We will get out from here at midnight! The defense counsel has questioned his witness for about four hours," said State Attorney Mr. Saraji. He asked the court to set another date for the hearing and we would start early in the afternoon.

The court ordered that the hearing be adjourned until 8 April 2021, and that I will remain remanded in custody.

On 8 April 2021, the court reconvened under the leadership of the magistrate Msafiri and attended by State Attorney Ms. Xaveria, I the defendant, and Advocate Mwakilima on behalf of my Advocate Faraji Mangula. The court clerk of the day was Zena.

The hearing began with the prosecutor informing the court that the case had been heard. But the magistrate who was hearing the case, Hon. Z. D. Laizer is on leave.

Before the adjournment, I told the court about the incident where I was beaten and badly injured by prison guards. I explained that my fellow inmates appointed me to present their case before guests who had come to the prison. The guests were members of the health committee of the Parliament of Tanzania, Commissioner General of Prison (CGP), Deputy Secretary

General for Ministry of Home Affairs, and other people. The head of Ruanda prison Regional Prison Officer (RPO) in Mbeya were not pleased with the information I presented to the visitors about the various grievances facing prisoners and detainees. He said that he would bring in a special squad or KM to teach us manners because we talked a lot when visitors come to the prison.

On the morning of 26 March 2021, the prison guards in their uniforms and wearing masks came in carrying clubs, whips, and electric wires. They hit us hard. They beat us as if they were killing snakes. I begged them not to hit me because I was sick, but they did not listen to me instead they bet me so hard with sticks on my shoulders and on my knees until I fell to the ground. I sustained major injuries that I couldn't walk for a week. As far as I know, I'm incarcerated as my case has no bail. I initially believed that prison is a safe place, but opposite is the case. Prison officers have no fear of law at all. They can beat prisoners as they wish. If there are crimes committed by inmates, why do the officers not handle the matter according to the legal procedures instead of beating people inhumanly? The torture took place in front of a Ruanda prison warden and some of his officers. Since, I am in prison on court bail, I ask the court to take action.

After my explanation, my Advocate Mwakilima emphasized by telling the court that 'Here' at the court, is the proper place to bring our grievances. Advocate Mwakilima added that the Regional Prison Officer (RPO) was a cruel man who does not respect human rights, and then expressed concern that I would be subjected to further tortures after filing a complaint of torture in court. "I believe that tonight our client will suffer a great deal." Said Advocate Mwakilima and added a request to the court, "I urge the court to issue a stern order otherwise the torture he will inflict today may even lead to his death."

For his part, the Prosecutor responded by saying that he had nothing to add as complaints against prisons were not related to the prosecution. The Prosecutor did not show any remorse for the torture I and other prisoners received at the hands of the prison officers neither did she show any curiosity, except for condemning the human rights abuses. Maybe she enjoyed it, or she is kind of carefree person.

The court, after my complaint ordered that with regard to the defendant's complaint that he has been tortured in prison, do hereby advises him to keep his complaint in writing through his attorney. The magistrate shall issue a warning order if required; the prison guards must ensure that the defendants are safe and treated fairly at all times in accordance with the laws of this country. The trial was adjourned on the same day until 22 April 2021, when it will come for mention. And I will remain in custody.

On 22 April 2021, the case was referred before Hon. Z. D. Laizer in the presence of state attorney Davice, I the defendant and clerk Mrs. Hosiana.

The State's Attorney told the court that the case had come to be head so we ask that you give us a date for the hearing. The court ruled that the date to continue hearing of this case should be 6 May 2021.

Before the Regional Resident Magistrate Hon. Z. D. Laizer, the session on 6 May 2021 was attended by the State Attorney Ms. Tengeneza, I the defendant, and the court clerk Ms. Luce. The State Attorney said we had come for the hearing but also the defendant's lawyer is in Dar es Salaam in session at the High Court. However, the defense had already filed a report of the absence of the defense counsel, and the court hearing was adjourned until 17 and 18 for a two-day hearing.

On 17 May 2021, before Hon. Z. D. Laizer, the session began with the attendance of State Attorneys Mr. Hebel and Ms. Tengeneza, I the defendant and the learned Advocate Faraji Mangula. The clerk of the court was Mrs. Luce.

State Attorneys Mr. Hebel Kihaka and Mrs. Tengeneza made it clear to the court that they have come for the hearing and that they are ready. Advocate Faraji Mangula also told the court that our side was ready.

The court began by reminding the prosecution of the exhibits of the defense witness number 1. I the Witness number 1 was also reminded that I was under oath, which I took on 25 March 2021.

After the introduction of the court attendance, State Attorney Mr. Kihaka stood for cross-examination against me…

State Attorney: *Mdude when questioned by your Advocate Mr. Faraji, you said you are a training officer for CHADEMA, tell the court what do you teach?*

Me: *I train new party leaders after they have been nominated or elected by the party.*

State Attorney: *At what level do you provide this training?*

Me: *I deal with the entire Nyasa region with five regions; Iringa, Njombe, Mbeya, Songwe and Rukwa.*

State Attorney: *How long have you been a human rights activist and when did you start?*

Me: *I have been an activist for over ten years. I started before 2009.*

State Attorney: *In your human rights movement, the sale of counterfeit drugs trafficking is part of that movement?*

Me: *Drug dealing is not part of the movement I am making.*

State Attorney: *Did you tell the court about the police following you without good reason?*

Me: *Yes, I did, as well as my kidnapping incidents planned and carried out by the police.*

State Attorney: *Do you remember the number of cases you have ever filed in court?*

Me: *I do not remember until I look in the relevant documents.*

State Attorney: *In one of your 2016 cases, you told the court that the police beat you with a 'fatuma' club—is it true or not true?*

Me: *It is true.*

State Attorney: *Did it break your bones?*

Me: *By God's grace it did not break a bone, but my legs were broken at the knees and ankles.*

State Attorney: *Did you tell the court where you were abducted on 4 May 2019?*

Me: *Yes, I told the court that I was on that day in Vwawa, Songwe region.*

State Attorney: *What areas were you abducted in Vwawa?*

Me: *I was abducted near the Songwe regional police station and NMB bank Vwawa Branch. It is about 200 meters from the Songwe RPC office.*

State Attorney: *What action did you take after the kidnappers arrived at your office?*

Me: *I made a loud shout, which made a lot of people to come, as the area is very busy with many people conducting their social economic works.*

State Attorney: *After the noise, did the people came forward for your rescue?*

Me: *People came out to save me. But the kidnappers managed to disperse them by firing shots into the air.*

State Attorney: *Are you sure your screaming for help reached the police station?*

Me: *I believe they heard because the police station is close to the place of incident but it was as if they conspired with the kidnappers.*

State Attorney: *How did the kidnappers introduce themselves to you?*

Me: *The kidnappers introduced themselves as police officers, and I asked them to let me call the Regional Police Commander to make me prove if they were sent to me. But instead of cooperating with me, they started slapping me and making derogatory remarks against me.*

State Attorney: *In your statement, you said the kidnappers beat you and you lost consciousness tell the court when did you regain consciousness?*

Me: *I gained consciousness on 8 May, when I was picked up by a good Samaritan in Inyala, Mbeya rural area.*

State Attorney: *Before you were found in Inyala did you know anything, which was going on your matter?*

Me: *No.*

State Attorney: *Now how did you know about the police refusal to open an investigation file as well as the Home Affairs minister's directives in parliament?*

Me: *I was having a press conference on my abduction. Before the meeting, I wanted to know what action the police have taken after the incident one, Mr. Masonga told me that the police have refused to open the file. Regarding the order of the Minister, I watched the parliamentary session via the 'YouTube' network.*

State Attorney: *You are complaining that so far, the kidnappers have not been arrested, true or false?*

Me: *It is true.*

State Attorney: *Did you identify the kidnappers?*

Me: *I could not identify any of those who abducted me.*

State Attorney: *Now, if you did not identify them how would the police have identified and arrested them?*

Me: *The police came to the hospital to interrogate me about the kidnappers. I gave them all the information they wanted and I also told them that the kidnappers took my phones and laptops. So, it is easy for them to track them through my mobile phones.*

State Attorney: *You said, you filed a lawsuit against IGP, AG, Songwe RPC, F.2820 D / CPL Nisile Mwaitenda and F.6960 DC Bashale, is it true or false?*

Me: *It is true.*

State Attorney: *Has the case been decided?*

Me: *This case is still being heard.*

State Attorney: *You said after you filed the case you started receiving threats, who were threatening you?*

Me: *I have been receiving so many threatening phone calls and every time I get a threatening call by new phone numbers. For example, one day while we were in the high court waiting to be called for the trial to begin, I met with an RPC from Songwe who told me to drop the case, as it would cause me more problems. I replied plainly that I have no fear of human being. I only fear God.*

State Attorney: *Why did you move from Vwawa in Songwe region to Mbeya?*

Me: *After being abducted and tortured, I had to stay close to the Mbeya Referral Hospital to ensure my health care.*

State Attorney: *When did you move to Mbeya?*

Me: *I moved to Mbeya from Vwawa in late 2019.*

State Attorney: *When were you arrested and who arrested you?*

Me: *I was arrested by ASP Siame and his accomplices on 10 May 2020.*

State Attorney: *Where were you taken to when you were arrested?*

Me: *They took me to the office for RCO Mbeya and on the same day at eight o'clock in the evening, they took me to the Central Police Station.*

State Attorney: *The sixth witness for the prosecution CPL Charles said you were the one who had the keys to your own house, Is it right?*

Me: *Not true, since the keys were with the police officers themselves.*

State Attorney: *Is it true that you searched the police officers before they entered your home for a search?*

Me: *Of course I did, but not to all. I searched only three of them and there were more than ten police officers.*

State Attorney: *Did you find anything with them in your search?*

Me: *No, I didn't find them with anything.*

State Attorney: *Is it true that the drugs were found in your residence?*

Me: *That is not true. What was found in my home was a khaki envelope suspected to have drugs.*

State Attorney: *What was in that envelope?*

Me: *I saw the envelope on the first time it was seized by the officers, and I was not given chance to see what was in it. The envelope has to date not been brought to court.*

State Attorney: *If you did not know what was in the envelope why did you sign the seizure form?*

Me: *I signed the form voluntarily because there were some of my belongings enlisted on it. There were more than twenty CDs with important information for my office activities .and two phones.*

State Attorney: *Were you able to identify the form here in court?*

Me: *Yes, I did identify the form but the khaki envelope that was said to have contained the drugs was not listed on the form nor was it brought to court.*

State Attorney: *Why is it important that the envelope be brought in?*

Me: *That khaki envelope would be a very important exhibit to be presented here in court. Its absence tarnishes all the evidence they gave on the prosecution. To make it worse is that I was not involved in the whole exercise of sending what they call a sample to the government chemist.*

State Attorney: *Do you remember the evidence of the state chemist given here in court, that he received items from ASP Siame and examined them?*

Me: *Yes, I remember, but not everything he said is true.*

State Attorney: *You said the indictment does not show the worth of the drugs. Is it a legal requirement?*

Me: *What amazes me is that the prosecution does not say the value of those drugs. And I don't think this is right.*

After the state attorney finished the cross-examination, it was the turn of my Advocate Faraji Mangula to undertake re-examination. After the correction, Adv. Mangula passed a motion to close the evidence presentation. "We ask that we close the evidence on our defense side. I ask the court that we bring our final submissions within fourteen days."

State Attorney Mr. Kihaka had no objections, further he added that they will also write a final submission of the prosecution details. The court therefore granted permission for the drafting of the submissions to be carried out as requested by the parties' lawyers. The court also ordered the submissions documents to be filed with the court on 31 May 2021, and on the same day, the case will be heard again. As for me, I will remain in custody.

On 31 May 2021, the case continued before Hon. Z. D. Laizer and attended by state attorney Mr. Davice, myself the defendant, learned Advocate Shilinde Swedi and court clerk Luce. State Attorneys Ms. Tengeneza and Mr. Davice told the court that they had submitted a written submission of the indictment to assist the magistrate in making the verdict. As well, Advocate Shilinde Swedi told the court, that they had also submitted their final defense statement.

Following court orders; one, that the verdict will be read on 14 June 2021, and the second, I the defendant will remain in custody. However, on that date, the court ruled that the sentence was still pending and that the verdict would be read on 28 June 2021.

VI
LIFE IN THE PRISON

"It is better to be a prisoner in the flesh and leave the mind free, than the imprisonment of the mind and leave the flesh free."
– Mdude M. Nyagali

It was on 13 May 2020, at four o'clock in the evening, one year after my abduction in my office in Vwawa, Mbozi in Songwe region. I was taken to the gates of the Ruanda prison in Mbeya city after being arraigned on bail in the Mbeya Resident Magistrate's Court. I remember one of the prison officers presents at the reception received and perused my charge sheet as per the prison order. The officer looked at the documents for a while and then turned to me reassuring me that this was a significant step for me. He seemed to be a miserable person but did not say what exactly was bothering him. Suddenly, he turned to me and asked me, "Mdude, when did you start this?" I could not answer him, but only tears welled up from my eyes in anguish.

He begged me to calm down and pray to God. He shook his head sadly, as he said to himself, *'the politics of this country have gotten worse.'* Then he conducted a search for me using a special search device, then followed the registration, and escorted me inside the prison cell. It was my second time in prison. The first time was in 2016 when I was charged with sedition, and I stayed in Vwawa prison for three days after the bail form was not finalized. Earlier, I had visited a Ruanda prison to see a former Mbeya MP, Hon. Joseph Mbilinyi, and Mr. Emmanuel Masonga, secretary of CHADEMA Nyasa zone. When I was imprisoned, these CHADEMA leaders had already left; now it is my turn to be visited, I thought so.

By the time I arrived in the prison, prisoners and detainees were already confined to their cells. It is a nationwide practice that prisoners and detainees in prisons are supposed to get in their cells at three o'clock in the evening, where the cell doors are locked from outside. Or in simple language, prisoners and detainees sleep at three o'clock in the evening and open at six o'clock in the morning—fifteen hours inside—and on weekends and holidays you can stay up to seventeen hours in cells.

The Prisoner Officer who received me told me that the prison administration had set aside cell 02 as a quarantine room, following the plunder of COVID-19 pandemic that was threatening the entire world. So, all new detainees are forced to be quarantined for fourteen days and then have their temperatures checked before being transferred to other cells or be sent to sickbay if they have signs of fever or flu.

Those prison cells have horrible structures. It is as if the authorities who decided to build the prisons agreed that the buildings should have a horrible shape. This prison was built during the colonial era in 1954 and even seems to reflect the atrocities perpetrated by the colonialists against Africans. They are old buildings that resemble old grain storage warehouses. At first, the door is only one, with small windows at the top through which one cannot see outside, and there is no enough ventilation. I was accompanied by the officer to cell number 02. With the keys in his hand, he knocked on the door as hard as he could with them, and then I heard a loud voice from inside the cell saying, "It is very safe, sir. We are locked-in sixty-seven prisoners, five are outside, sir. Cell Number 02, sir."

But that is the prison system, that when a prison officer knocks on a door, Nyapara begins by saying that it is safe inside and then mentions the number of prisoners and detainees inside the cell and those who were released for some reason.

As soon as the cell door was opened, the officer ordered me to enter, which I did. I was stunned when I saw the number of people inside and as I looked at the size of the cell, why is it so small and so populated! I was shocked. The size of the cell is about 14 feet wide because two six-foot mattresses are arranged by either side leaving a small space of about 2 feet at the middle. The height of the cell is about 50 feet. People are filled with compact like ants. There is no enough air and the light is dim. People are like animals; they are lying on their side with each other.

I thought to myself, "Now what's the point here about Corona if people are stuck like this?" As these questions pondered in my heart, I suddenly heard a voice calling for me to squat down. "Who do think you are to stand up while your fellows are asleep!" I obeyed to that command immediately. A young man who seemed to have authority in the cell squeezed his foot to separate the sleeping men and gave a command to get me a tiny space to sleep. He then called me and said, "Bro come and sleep here already the space has been found." It's a problem! That space I was told has been found is enough for the foot to just enter and not the whole body. Instead of anger and rage now, I was in immeasurable surprise. I struggled with myself and forced myself into that position, and eventually, I became part of the influx of people.

While squeezed amidst my fellow inmates, bells were ringing in my mind as to how will I be able to overcome this new life in prison. I was wearing a facemask that made my face look ugly. I know there are people in there who knew me but because of the mask, they didn't recognize me. The sound of the cell radio was audible and now a news bulletin was announced. I heard one report about me, "CHADEMA cadre Mdude Nyagali has been arraigned before the Mbeya Resident Magistrate's Court on charges of…"

The man who seemed to be the leader in the cell slapped the wall as a sign to command silence. Suddenly there was a great silence in whole cell. Then the man made a proclamation for the people to be quiet. The radio continued to announce that Mdude Nyagali had been sent to Ruanda prison as his case was not bailable. So, the master in charge of the cell said that if Mdude was brought here to prison he must be in cell number 02 as he was in quarantine. He asked aloud if Mdude was in the cell, and I answered, "I'm here." He approached me and told me to take off my mask so that he could recognize me. I took off my mask. I saw that he was very happy, so he ordered his subordinates to keep Mdude from being 'censored' and instead to sleep where V.I.P sleeps.

To my surprise, I thought the so-called V.I.P is another room! But it is right in there. It is at the corner near the wall. The only difference is this that the small mattresses, about six by two and a half feet long, are not worn out, and are slept on by two people each. That is the honor of V.I.P. When the 'census' or 'bush' side, about four or more people are sleeping on a mattress of the size of six by two and a half feet, and the mattresses themselves are very much worn and sometimes non-existent, so they have to sleep on the floor with no sheets or blanket to cover them. The occupants who sleep at 'censuses' are weak and powerless and have no rank in and out of the cell. In prison language, people who sleep at census or bush are called 'farmers.' It must be considered that in Tanzania 'farmers' are the lowest people than the rest. So, the name 'farmer' as used in the prison refers to as 'inferiority.' All prison mattresses are the same size.

Later, in the night after the prayers service, the prisoner in charge (PIC) called all eleven of us who had entered that day to teach us the rules of living in the prison as well as to introduce us to the officials found inside the prison. We arrived and squatted on the edge of his mattress, and he began to deliver his sermon to us. He said that the prison warden and all the prison officers are people who deserve respect as long as you are inside the prison. If you are called by any prison officer, you should respond with discipline and with a loud voice saying 'Yes Sir,' while running towards the one who called you. When you get to the officer, you must squat to listen to what he called you for.

Any prison officer, whether high or low, is called a 'Sir' or 'Master' or 'Father' or 'Elder.' Whenever called within the prison you must respond by saying 'Yes, sir' loudly. It is a serious mistake to clap in the cell, as the clap is made by the PIC and the Nyapara alone, as a call for people to remain silent in order to present certain information that will be presented by any leader within the cell. Alternatively, the applause may be done during worship, or it may be applauded by Nyapara at dawn and at bedtime. That is, if you hear a clap in evening it means calm down and sleep, even if you are not sleepy, and when you hear a slap in the morning, it means wake up and queue in line to get out even if you were still asleep.

After the ranks of prison officers, the next rank is the Chief Nyapara of the entire prison fort. Chief Nyapara of the fort is a very respectable man inside the prison even though it is a fact that he too is a prisoner. He is a strong and influential man. Often the prisoners who get this position are those who are strong and physically built up. In short, he is a prison lord and is the only person who is given the honor of sleeping on a bed of two and a half by six feet in a cell while the rest of them sleep on mattresses laid on the floor. As with prison officers, when you are summoned by the Chief Nyampara then you must respond by shouting, 'Yes, sir' as you approach him politely and as you approach him you squat, waiting to hear his voice. The main task of the Chief Nyampara of the fort is to co-operate with prison officials to ensure that the activities of prisoners, both inside and outside the prison are carried out and stability is maintained.

From the *Chief Nyampara* of the fort, the next rank is for the 'common nyaparas.' These have a number of responsibilities, one of which is overseeing the inmates to ensure that prison functions are carried out on time and in the intended manner. These *common nyamparas* are given mattresses inside the cell to sleep on their own, but not in bed like the Chief Nyapara. Compassionately, if they are sympathetic, then they can take any 'farmer' or 'census' and give him a chance to sleep on his mattress on the side of the V.I.P.

After the usual narcissists, the next rank is the 'red tapes.' In civilian life, when you hear that a person is a 'red tape' you despise him or her, but in prison, it is a title desired by most prisoners. The main function of these red tapes is to encourage people to work in prisons. They move in groups like wolves, arresting people in prisons, collecting them, and taking them to toilet cleaning, kitchen, field, watering vegetables gardens, etc. If you want to know how notorious these chaps are, express yourself as an inmate who can't do works.

Beside those titles, then you go into the cell the titles continue. In the cell, the loudest person is the 'main cell nyampara,' who is chosen by the other nyampara of that cell or may be appointed by the 'Chief Nyampara' of the fort. That is, the Chief Nyampara of the fort may appoint the 'main cell nyamparas' of the entire prison cells. After all those, who follow in command or power are the common nyamparas. Under them the next rank is the PIC, who was the one giving us the lesson. The task of the PIC is to teach detainees and prisoners how to live in the prison and to introduce the guests to the cell nyamparas, and then the guests are ordered to salute them as a sign of respect.

That PIC are selected by the cell nyampara inside the cell, and one must be a prisoner and another, a detainee. Saluting is a procedure I have never liked, but on the first day, everyone must do it. The PIC led us to five cell nyamparas and every time you came to one you salute by being led by the PIC. He will begin by asking, 'Do you see this one?' And you respond, 'Yes Sir!' Then he asks you, 'This is a government's nyampara, what does he deserve?' You answer, 'Respect! Sir.' Then he asks again, 'If you make a mistake?' You answer, *"Mbata or fifteen strokes!"* After that, you are sent to another cell nyampara to start and follow the instructions again.

The next rank after the PIC is the 'health master.' His job is to make sure he prepares drinking water in the cell every day, teaches visitors how to drink water in prison inspects unclean people who do not bathe and washes and shaves hair all parts of the body. A health master has the authority to inspect any prisoner or detainees. If you are found violating one of the prison rules, then you will be taken to the duty nyampara, who will order the cell nyampara to bend you over and unbutton your shirt, and you will receive several mbatas. Mbatas are those Maasai shoes that are carved using scrap car tires. So, if you hear an order being issued you should be beaten and you should know that you are going to be beaten by using Maasai shoes. At the arrival to jail, you will be told that if you break the rules there, you will be beaten fifteen times.

From the health master, then the next title is 'Kabarabara.' Due to overcrowding in the cells, 'Kabarabara' is tasked to ensure that the tiny path that remains in the middle after laying the mattresses is protected so that no one puts anything that will cause inconvenience to the path users when going to the toilet. When you enter and are locked in a cell, 'Kabarabara' will collect all shoes and put them in a bag, and then put them in the closet due to lack of space.

The next title is 'Cleaner.' Tasks to this person are a little bit heavy. First, one of his tasks is to teach guests how to use the toilet. And the 'Cleaner' mattress is about 4 feet from the toilet hole. There are times when you may be defecating, and the 'Cleaner' will continue to eat food regardless of the bad smell that comes out while you are defecating. Toilet unstopping is a common practice for 'Cleaner', who insert a hand into the toilet sink without wearing gloves or any precautions to find out what caused the toilet to clog. If you want to see how fierce the 'Cleaner' is, use the toilet badly.

A person who does not have any rank in prison is called a 'farmer.' Many people struggle to find any position to earn a living from sleeping in the V.I.P., not being forced to work hard in prison, and even better opportunity to use a toilet. Toilets are not enough, so only those officials and celebrities are allowed to bathe in the cell. Some take shower using outside toilets after they are opened in the morning.

Beside the specified ranks, every person imprisoned under the age of thirty must be in one of the 'gangs.' When you talk about a gang inside a prison, it means a task force made up of several prisoners under the supervision of prison officers and the chief nyampara of the fort for performing certain tasks. The day you are incarcerated as a prisoner and registered is the day to be assigned to your work gang.

Gangs depend on the prison you are in. In some prisons, there is a 'brick gang', whose job is to produce bricks for construction or sale. Then there is the 'gang building.' This is a group of prisoners who are involved in the construction of buildings, and often the prisoners of this gang are those construction technicians or anyone with knowledge of those works. The 'sanitation gang' is a clean-up gang, especially in the suburbs, in public offices such as courts, councils, and so on. Many prisoners prefer to be in the 'hygienic gang' because they have the opportunity to meet people whom, they may ask and get money or food from. Prisoners see the 'hygiene gang' as the most luxurious gang and getting a place in that gang is not a small task. The most feared gang is the 'farm gang,' which is a farmers' gang. And the cultivation itself is not voluntary but by force and many sticks from the *nyamparas* and *red tapes*. I have personally seen this from the prisoners as they come out of the field, taking off their shirts and showing me their backs torn with whips.

That is how I started my new life in prison by being introduced to the officials as well as being taught the principles of life in prison.

***

Just two days after entering the prison, the Mbeya Regional Prisons Officer (RPO) arrived and ordered the prison officers to search for me and take me to where he was. Nyapara started calling me out loud. I responded as was taught 'Yes Sir!' and ran quickly to the prison chief's office, where I was directed to go. When I arrived, I found the RPO with the prison warden as well as the senior prison officers in Mbeya region. So quietly and politely, as was taught, I squatted and waited for the call.

The RPO ordered me to take off my mask so that he could see me better, and after that he began to explain how he knew me. That I have been insulting President Magufuli on social media and that I have been involved in forming groups and training for insulting President Magufuli. He continued that my intention is to make the president appear to be incompetent in the international community. He rather said that I have acquired these trainings in Germany. I responded by saying that all that information was untrue as I never have traveled abroad and that the immigration department does not have any information of my traveling abroad. He ordered me to remain silent and claimed that his other work outside the prison, which is unknown to me. He went on saying that even Mandela used fake names and fake passports, which was not issued, by his country, so even immigration department could not get his information.

I told the RPO the case that brought me was not that. He became very angry and told me to keep quiet or else he would order officers to beat me up. He ordered that I first be shifted from quarantine cell, where I had to stay for fourteen days, and then be moved to another cell, as in the quarantine cell, one was not allowed to do any work as they were on the verge of symptoms of COVID-19 disease. How much hatred has blinded this RPO for not caring about the lives of other people he does not know!

The RPO continued to instruct the prison warden and other officers to ensure that I was kept very busy inside the prison, from watering vegetables, sweeping, flushing toilets, cleaning the kitchen, and washing dishes to make me exhausted, and that I should always go to bed with my tongue sticking out like that of a hunting dog. He concluded by saying that even President Magufuli would be happy to hear Mdude is 'walking on 90 speeds' in prison. The meaning of 'walking on 90 speeds' in prison is to work continuously without rest from six o'clock in the morning when the cell opens until three o'clock in the afternoon when you are locked inside the cell.

And in fact, that day I was moved from the quarantine cell and sent to cell number 11. The next morning after taking porridge, I was followed by *red tapes* who wanted me to go and water the vegetables. I warned them not to get involved in a crisis that could bring them greater problems than they had in prison. They were afraid and left. They then sent a report to the Nyampara, and the Nyampara reported the matter to prison officer in charge with security matters at the prison. The officer came and, while talking to me, I was surrounded by Nyamparas and red tapes waiting for an order from the Prison officer to tell them to do anything against me.

The officer asked me why I had refused to work as a vegetable gardener when there was no super-star in prison. I replied that I was incarcerated and I knew my rights; the law protects me from working until the court finds me guilty and orders me to serve a sentence. I continued to insist that if they wanted me to work, then they would wait for me to be arrested and tell the Director of Public prosecutions (DPP) to hurry up and complete the investigation of my case. But also, anyone who touches me by beating me or forcing me to work then my lawyers will die with him in court. After making those statements, the officer seemed to understand the matter and ordered the *Nyamparas* and the *red tapes* to go for other tasks and just leave me alone.

I did not want to just defend myself but also began to defend other people as well. People loved me and gave me many names; some called me the 'president' of the prison, and others called me the 'man of missiles,' that is the man who fired missiles. You know the people in prisons have a language that sometimes you may not understand. For example, gays inside the prison are called the names of female artists and beauties here or abroad especially in Europe and the United States. There is Shilole, there is Wema Sepetu, there is Rihanna, and there is Beyonce, Amba Lulu, and others. Those are some of the names given to gays in prison. These gays are collectively referred to as the *'prison babes.'*

The mental patient is called 'number four' as they occupy cell number four. The delicious food that comes from outside the prison is called 'Cha kuloa.' It should also be noted that any food that comes out of prison is always tasty and given great respect. A bag, package, or any other storage bag is called a 'Shako.'

There are people called 'Warombo' people. Those are people who have a comfortable life and spend money on self-sufficiency by buying food outside the prison and sometimes bribe Nyamparas to avoid being harassed in prison and be given certain privileges including sleeping at V.I.P. It is a common occurrence for manyaparas to cling to 'Warombo.' In short, no warombo sleeps in 'censuses' or 'bushes.'

Some are 'Maoderi', these are the helpers of Nyamparas or celebrities. They help to wash their boss's dishes, wash his clothes, go to the food queue on behalf of his boss, and carry the luggage of the boss brought by his visitors who come to see him in prison, such as soap, food, juice, bread, and so on. For all the work they do, the *maoderi* are paid for pieces of soap and sometimes get lucky to be given food from outside the prison by his boss such as rice, potato chips, and so on.

That is prison life. It is a very difficult, but if you are told, you will laugh instead of crying. Happy days are the four annual religious festivals that we get rice and football days. In prison, there are eight football teams. There are Yanga, Simba, Toto Africa, Manchester Utd, Lipuli, Tukuyu Stars, Prison, and Mbeya City. There is a league sponsored by people from outside the prison, and the winner of the league is given jerseys, shoes, and soap. The women also have their games, but their area is small, and the separating fence is too high to see each other. At least that eating rice and playing football are the things to laugh at in the midst of a life of suffering.

***

I remember the day I suffered a lot in prison. This is the day I was badly beaten by the Special Squard in Swahili call 'Kikosi Maalumu' or simply *KM*. The saga began on 6 March 2021 in a Ruanda prison when we received a heavy national visit. The visitors were the Deputy Secretary General of the Ministry of Home Affairs, members of the health committee for Parliament of Tanzania and the Commissioner General of Prisons—— (CGP) in Tanzania. According to the visitors, they were paying visits to all prisons across the country, collecting information about prisoners and detainees' welfare.

The visitors asked prisoners and detainees to suggest the names of two people who could present their grievances on behalf of the entire prison. I was recommended by an elder named Akimu Mwakalinga. The old man has been a 'Prison fighter' for ten years; he has been in prison, meaning that he was fighting for the rights of prisoners inside the prisons. This task of defending rights of prisoners has led to his being shifted from one prison to another. The old man and I presented the grievances faced by detainees in the prison, and the guests promised to work on them.

One day in the morning after the visit, the bell rang to indicate there was something wrong. So, as usual, we gathered in the field waiting for the call. There came the prison warden along with the RPO. They showed great anger on their faces. I did not know what their anger was about, but I knew of it when they started talking. On several occasions, they verbally attacked me and warned me that I should focus on my case rather than on defending prisoners and detainees whom I did not know.

The officers blamed my fellow prisoners and the detainees for making my head big because when I presented their grievances to the guests, they were cheering and clapping to me. They kept insisting that it was time to bring a 'special squad'— KM into the prison to beat us because we pretended to know how to speak. The RPO concluded by saying that on that day, he would order KM to beat Mdude on the testicles to death, and he would write a statement, and then he would see whom the detainees would be talking to. Then they close the meeting and left.

I thought they were only threatening us, but Mr. Akimu Mwakalinga, who was also the target, said he has ten years of experience with prisons. He says he was being transferred to prisons for raising concerns or claiming any rights within the prison. He went on to say that, in short, the prisons do not like challenges, and it is true they can bring KM, but he insisted not to be afraid because he has been severely beaten by KM before and is still living. Then Mr. Akimu took off his shirt and showed me his back. I saw horrible scars on old Akimu's back caused by canings. There are strips all over his back.

On 26 March 2021, the day of President Magufuli's funeral, a strange thing happened to detainees and prisoners. But I was targeted.

We were awakened very early in the morning before six o'clock, unlike the other days they would wait until we had finished listening to the news on BBC. Soon a group of 'special squad'—KM came in wearing masks to hide their faces. The beatings began inside the cell as everyone rushed to the door to save his life. If you succeeded to go through the door, you were ordered to run fast without looking on any side to the playing field while being whipped with stripes, high-tension wires, and clubs on the back. Still on the field, they drew a small circle and demanded that more than a thousand people enter the circle while we took off our clothes and held them in our hands. Certainly, there was a great congestion as people laid on each other, and those KMs beat us on the heads and other parts of the body with sticks and whips. Many people lost consciousness. They were carried and laid aside, and then the beating continued to the rest of us.

Prison officers working in this fort were not allowed inside the prison during the operation. They beat us like mad dogs.

Many were injured and lost consciousness, but those beaters did not care. We were really beaten. One of the officers with a mask over his face approached me and asked my why is my leg so swollen. I replied that I was in pain and not only on the foot but also had head problems since the time I had the abduction incident. He asked me, "Are you Mdude?" I answered, "Yes." He commanded me to follow him. He took me to the inner prison clinic or Sickbay, told me to stay there, and then closed the door and left. Then at Sickbay, there was a large window where I could see the whole area of the playing ground where the beatings were going on. The other patients and I poked out through the window.

My colleagues continued to be beaten for more than two hours. They were exhausted. When they finished, the callers started looking for me. Everybody was beaten to say where I was! They refused to do so because I was so supportive of their efforts when a large government and judicial delegation arrived at the prison. When the beaters hit them hardest one of the inmates said, "You will kill us for no reason, Mdude is in Sickbay."

They followed me to sickbay and took me out to where other people were. While outside, they told me I was harassing the government. I was brought to prison but could not calm down and pretended to be Mandela now let them show me. They started beating me, torturing me. They caused terrible pains by beating me randomly with clubs and wires on all parts of my body. I have never seen or been told of this kind of beating. It is more than killing a snake. That is a well-fed 'giant' throws more than fifty sticks in one minute on one shoulder. Then he repeats to the back of the same victim, then on knees and arms. The pain subsided. I could not evade, protect myself or fold my arms anymore. I just stared at them. I saw death coming towards me.

On that day, I certainly saw death. Suddenly, from the distance, I saw people stretching out their arms and receive me at the coolest place. It was a true illustration that the spirit has being separated from the body. They laid me down. Immediately, they began to press me with hot water and salt. I felt fast asleep.

When I woke up, I found that my attendants were my fellow prisoners and the KM had left for a long time. Prison security officer came and ordered that I be taken to Mbeya Referral Hospital, but the detainees and prisoners refused and said they rather see me die at their hands than die at the hands of my tormentors. I had difficulty in walking because of severe pain in my leg and hips. It took me a whole month to get back to normal.

As is my custom, I do not accept defeat or oppression from anyone, no matter how powerful. I filed a complaint with the court, demanding that the court take action if it did not agree with the prison action. As word spread on social media, the situation worsened on the part of the prison chief and the RPO. They started phoning my lawyer Faraji Mangula, wanting to sit down with him to talk and resolve the issue out of court. Later, the RPO followed me to the prison and apologized for the unlawful beating by his team. And I gave him conditions that in order to pardon him, he should publicly apologize in front of all the prisoners and detainees in the entire prison. He agreed and did so and I forgave him and informed my lawyer as well.

***

During the four hundred and fourteen days I was in prison, I faced many challenges and tried to learn as much as I could. I chose to use my suffering as an opportunity to learn new things. I sought information from every available source, including prisoners and detainees, my lawyers, and even the prison officers. One of the things I learnt was about overcrowding in various prisons in our country. By the way, the detainees are much more in our prisons than prisoners are. It is fair to say that Tanzanian prisons are there for more detainees than prisoners are. For example, in Ruanda prison, where I was, which is also a zonal prison in the Southern Highlands, has a capacity of four hundred people, and the average capacity of each cell is up to twenty-five people. But due to overcrowding, the prison is forced to hold more than thousand people. Of that number, detainees are estimated to be seven hundred and fifty, or three-quarters. By that calculation, a cell with a capacity of twenty to twenty-five people is populated by seventy to hundred people.

Sometimes, you can't even find your way to the toilet because the Nyamparas are forced to arrange people to sleep on the cell path due to overcrowding. If you succeed in going to the toilet, when you return you will find that, the space you were lying on has disappeared due to the crowd. Then you will have to lie down on top of others. Imagine, how can a person get fresh air in such an environment?

Ventilation system is very poor. Windows are small and high enough to make the air inside the cell heavier. This condition causes some prisoners and detainees to fall sick. Many get severe attack by hypertension, asthma, or even lose consciousness. I was curious to know the long-term effects prisoners and detainees get out of this tragedy. But I could not find any statistics. I have no doubt that there are long-term health effects that prisoners, inmates, and detainees experience because of the heavy and dirty air they breathe in at the cell. Worse still, if someone suddenly falls ill or loses consciousness, those inside the cell are forced to knock on the heavy door, as is the only way to call the prison officers guarding from outside the cell. When an officer arrives, he won't open the door immediately, but the Nyampara will explain the problem to him about the problem that has caused him make a call. Then the officer will report to the administration so that he gets permission to open the cell door. Then he returns to open the cell door and take the sick person to the dispensary popularly known as *Sick Bay* or a prison clinic for first aid. In addition, efforts to alert officers that there is something needing their attention requires a Nyampara to kick the cell door so hard but still they may delay for even hours to come. I was very much afraid that there was a day when I will witness deaths. Thank God that for all the days I was in prison, no one lost life in the cell, although I was told that deaths were common inside the cells.

What hurts most is that, despite the suffering caused by the poor cell environment, on the day you go to court to follow up with your case, the state prosecutor tells the court the investigation is incomplete. The court will then adjourn the case regardless of how long the case has taken. For example, there is a case of a Mozambican citizen named Simon Eugenio Faducum, number PI.29 / 2010, whose investigation was not completed from 2010 to 2021. The man has been in prison for more than a decade without a court sentence. At a law week meeting in February 2021 held in prison, I interviewed a senior State Attorney, Mr. Saraji, along with former Mbeya Regional Commissioner, wanting to know why Simon's case has not ended for ten years. Their response was that the Mozambican citizen did not know *Swahili* or *English* and instead spoke only *Portuguese*. That is why his case was delayed. They went on to say that now that he has learnt Swahili his case will be given priority and that they would ensure that the case will be completed in 2021. Unsatisfied with their response, I asked again that in prison there were over a hundred Ethiopians who does not know Swahili or English, there were also two other Mozambican citizens who also did not know English or Kiswahili, but their cases were over and they were serving prison sentences. Why is Simon the only one standing trial by the language barrier? The response was the same that they were working on the challenge.

There are many other examples of such cases. However, one of the main reasons for the overcrowding in prisons is that of detectives taking too long to incomplete investigations.

Why does the investigation of the cases take so long? And why does a person suffer incarceration for so long. It may take more than ten years to investigate a simple case. The quick answer to why cases take so long is that most cases in this category are cases of forgery or economic sabotage. When some police officers find that there is no evidence to convict a suspect due to the nature of the case, they decide to imprison him on the grounds of incomplete investigation. But again, so many people are in prison following their refusal to pay bribes to the investigators and prosecutors.

Another answer as to why some cases take so long is police investigator's laziness and lack of competence or investigative equipment. It is very difficult for the Tanzanian police force to conduct a criminal investigation without torturing the suspect to force one to agree with the crime alleged to have committed even if he was not involved. That is the most relied-upon method by the police. In Ruanda prison, I did a little research just to find that out of ten murder cases, eight suspects were acquitted after a court dismissed the suspect's police questions Statement provided at the police station due to legal limitations. The main reasons for the dismissal at the court were the accused being beaten and tortured thus failing to provide statement information voluntarily, the questions statement being taken out of time and the accused not being given the right to have a witness or lawyer at the time of writing the statement.

For example, a murder may be committed and if the police do not find the culprit, they can rampantly arrest anyone, or if they arrest one murder suspect they will give him all other murder cases that occurred in the area. A person could be arrested for stealing a television set but whilst in remand will be given a charge on murder he even does not about.

I have living examples of cases like this, one of which is three young men I found in prison facing six murder cases. The youths are Adam Bryson, Oscar Elias, and Benjamin Sylvester, who according to their statement, they were brought to court in early 2020 facing one murder case, which is case PI.5 / 2020. But one month later, while in prison they were brought another indictment PI.6 / 2020. As of July 2020, they had been charged with six counts of murder, namely PI.13 / 2020, PI.20 / 2020, PI.81 / 2020 and PI.61 / 2020. Most surprisingly, the case PI.05 / 2020 and the late PI.20 / 2020 is one. That is, one deceased has two cases filed against the same suspects. The youths agreed to write a statement stating that they were responsible for the killings on both sides despite the fact that the deceased was one in both cases. On the day of the law week meeting at the prison, I asked the Mbeya district commissioner of criminal investigations OC-CID if the suspects killed the deceased and then the deceased was resurrected and they killed him again or how was the deceased killed twice? I am not defending the suspects because I do not know if they actually killed or not. Only the court has the responsibility to ascertain the truth. But there are questions in some of these cases and prove the limited capacity of the Tanzanian police force in undertaking investigations. After my questions and comments, a week later one of the six cases were dismissed.

Another guy by the name of Bahati Kuve was arrested in 2017 and his murder case was opened by the number PI.21/2017. According to the laws of our country murder cases are among the most unconventional cases. So, after the indictment Mr. Bahati was forced to be held in prison. In 2019, the court acquitted Mr. Bahati after a lack of evidence in his case but he was arrested in court immediately by the police and then taken to Mbalizi Mbeya police station where he was detained for two days and then was brought to court pending a new murder case, PI.15/2018. Mr. Bahati is alleged to have committed the crime in 2018 while he was still in prison since his arrest on another murder charge in 2017. The question to ask is whether Mr. Bahati escaped from prison, and went to kill someone outside, and then returned to prison? All of these questions should be used to question the loyalty and ability of the police to investigate and prosecute cases competently and professionally.

All of this is due to the police's failure to conduct a thorough investigation into various incidents. It is as if the detective police officers are forcing lies as long as they are seen working in front of their superiors.

The courts, in turn, cannot avoid the blame for contributing to the overcrowding in prisons. There are times when the court fails to differentiate itself from the state prosecutor's office— DPP, by accepting every argument brought before the court about incomplete investigations. Another issue is the court is accused of delaying the issuance of case documents after the accused is imprisoned. That when a prisoner wants to appeal, he must have a judgment and the proceedings of his case, but it takes probably months until years to get those documents so that he can appeal against the sentence. Sometimes appeals are rejected because they are time-barred. There is also a challenge for the court to keep the documents. The prisoners may file an intention to appeal after the verdict, but on the day of submission of his appeal, he will be told that his intention note is not available.

A vivid example is on Mr. Khaleed Lusambo and his colleagues, whose case number is 50/2001. In 2002, they were sentenced to life imprisonment before Sumbawanga resident magistrate's court. They appealed, and the high court later struck their appeal. Since the high court dismissed their appeal, they have not received a copy of the decision on the appeal so that they can appeal to the Court of Appeal. They have twenty years in prison and do not know their fate. Mr. Khaleed says he has lodged a complaint several times with the registrar of courts but has been informed that their case file is missing and they are still searching for it. When will our courts begin to see themselves as the most important instruments of justice, hope, and relief to the people?

There has been a serious problem of food and shelter in our prisons. Fortunately, for me, inside the prison, I met some prisoners from various prisons in the country, and we exchanged greetings. I found out that the challenges of all prisons in the country are very similar. Many complains that food, water, and shelter are inadequate. Who has said that the punishment of a prisoners and detainees is to deprive them from getting basic human services? Although the prison I was in has clean running water all the time, but there are other problems like food and shelter. According to our prison system, if you are a prisoner or detainee, you will get food once a day after drinking one cup of porridge in the morning. That is, from the time cell is opened at 6.30 in the morning, you are going to queue for tasteless corn porridge. Don't ask for snacks or sugar; that's a strange thing in prison. After taking the morning porridge, you will have to wait until one o'clock in the afternoon when the food bell rings. You are supposed to queue for lunch, and everyone will be given one plate of stiff porridge and half a cup of beans. Having eaten, whether satisfied or not, you will wait until three o'clock to be locked up in a cell to sleep until the next morning. There is no another food except stiff porridge with beans from January to December. The only day we change diet is during Islamic and Christian religious holidays if good Samaritans bring rice and meat to the prison. Note that only good Samaritans will be allowed to bring rice and meat.

There are few detainees who are able to buy food from outside the prison. There is no specific diet for people living with HIV-AIDS and other diseases. Seldom do they get little food at ten o'clock in the morning, popularly known as 'shtua.' They are given a little porridge in a cup with beans soup.

In terms of accommodation, the biggest problem is the shortage of mattresses and blankets in our prisons. Mattresses are very old and should not be used by human beings. Don't be surprised to find prisoners and detainees lying on the floor, mending small pieces of mattress that have been cut off and broken into cells during a sleep. Blankets are not enough; many are forced to sleep without a blanket. Now imagine the cold of Mbeya, Songwe, Iringa, and Njombe; that is the life of an animal. This is happening to people in this twenty-first century. It is a serious human rights violation in Tanzania's prisons.

Beating and torturing suspects before being brought to court has become a common practice by the police force. Most victims of such tragedies are those with criminal cases. In Ruanda prison alone, of more than seven hundred detainees, more than five hundred whom I interviewed told me that they were tortured by the police officers to force them agree to the allegations and write a question statement police wanted. Some of them were imprisoned due to the strangeness of the court environment, which made them unable to express themselves freely and properly.

The Mbeya regional police officers are well aware of my reprimands for getting to the prison to collect inmates' grievances. I warned them to stop beating and torturing people during the interviews and instead to investigate without hurting suspected persons. I reminded them by giving out living examples from prison, only the rape suspects are among the few who are not beaten during interviews, and they are free to write question statements. Even at their refusal, but a large percentage of rape cases lead to imprisonment rather than other cases following availability of more evidences and free witnesses. I clearly told police officers that if the suspect refuse to write down the details on question statements, they should gather enough evidence instead of beating them. Unfortunately, my advice was not taken seriously, as many of the suspects who continued to be incarcerated in the prison complained of being tortured by the police.

In my personal experience of police brutality, as a result of being held at many police stations, from Vwawa in Songwe region, Mbeya, the main post office Dar es Salaam, to Oysterbay station in Dar es Salaam—I am persuaded to believe that torturing suspects is a system instituted by the entire Tanzanian police force, contrary to the laws of the country. For example, at Vwawa – Songwe, there is a torture chamber, as described earlier, called *Guantamo Bay*. I was dragged and tortured into that room. At the Mbeya police headquarters, there is a torture chamber called the 'Garage.' When you are inside the detention room of the Mbeya police station, if you manage to look through the upper right windows you will see this torture room. At the main Post Office and Oysterbay station, these rooms are called *garages* as in Mbeya. At Vwawa, Posta and Oysterbay stations, the detachment is called *anti-robbery* but in Mbeya their torture unit is called *Doria 8*.

When some suspects are arrested before they are questioned, they are first taken to a torture chamber, stripped, handcuffed, and then hung on a rope around their legs and arms, followed by beatings on various parts of the body. I was badly beaten on my feet, knees, and buttocks. There are others who, according to them, were subjected to more brutal acts, such as inserting objects in anus, or a bicycle spoke is inserted into the penis. Some inmates showed me the scars from the nails plugged on their shanks. These were pierced with hammered nails, in the same manner as former Hai district commissioner Lengai Ole Sabaya and his gang were doing. It is possible that there is an exchange of these torturing techniques and experiences among the various torture forces within the police force. I am not sure if this persecution is found in any other country except Tanzania. At the end of the day, the suspect decides to comply with police orders so that he will not continue to be tortured.

I remember an incident at Mbeya Central Police Station in May 2020. While incarcerated with other suspects we heard loud noises outside the remand cell. We poked through small windows to see what the noise was about. It was a woman's noise. Tears came through my eyes after seeing the garage men beating a woman accused of killing her husband in collaboration with a traditional healer. First, the woman was tortured by male police officers, then she was stripped naked, and she was beaten until she defecated and then the police officers forced her to lick her own stool. It is indeed the brutality perpetrated by the police, which may make one feel that these guys are not born from ordinary mothers. You may feel it is a fictional story, but it is a fact that I have witnessed with my own eyes and heard by my own ears. I was devastated that day and sat there thinking about the brutality of these creatures; I could not sleep. This brutality is often carried out at night.

Mbeya regional detainees complains is about the *eighth patrol, or Doria 8* of torture. They claim that if you were taken to *Inyara* by the torturers of the eighth patrol and come back breathing, you must thank God. Many people die in agony, and their corpses are thrown into the deep abyss where they will never be seen. I received this information about the torture of the patrol 8 from my friend Emma Bebabeba, who is one of the victims of police brutality and is now a prisoner in Ruanda prison. I am still trying to find out the truth about this natural pit in the area, and if the police dump bodies of those dies in their hands.

***

My Advice

Following the tragedies as I have explained above, it is with my deep concern that I should provide advice to the government to take a number of steps in making laws enforceable and thus comply with international human rights resolutions.

Criminal Procedures Act 1985 (CPA) is so outdated. With it, the police force cannot be checked while conducting investigations. They can do whatever they wish including torturing suspects contrary to the law itself, and thus violating basic human rights to the people, they attended.

The government should draft amendments to guide the police force to do all their investigative tasks adhering to this act, short of which they will also be punishable by the law. Rights of suspects should be well explained and checked. By today's police conduct, it is as if the law is silent on what might be done if he violates the right of a detainee. All in all, the person alleged to have committed crime depends on the police officer's mercy on his/her fate.

The reason for the delay in the investigation is clearly based on these loopholes. I, therefore, advise the government to include in the amendment a placement of the time limit in investigating cases. Again, investigation should be taken confidentially, thereafter, an arrest may be made. Short of which many people will continue being arrested and imprisoned thus causing overpopulation in our prison cells. It is inhuman to detain a person for years just to come into conclusion that the person is pleaded not guilty.

The government should in the amendment set a clause(s) which will bar courts of law to receive a case whose investigation is incomplete.

There should also be placed time limit for hearing of cases before the court. Delay in the court has as well contributed so much in the overcrowding of inmates in the prisons.

Police force officers have proved negligence and incompetent in completing investigative tasks. I therefore advise for an amendment be drafted that will bring major changes to the force by separating investigation department from police force. There should formed a department away from police force unit, which will deal with investigation only. Just like, it is to USA's

FBI. This department should be populated by well-trained persons and be provided with modern gear to aid them complete investigations professionally. That the students who registered in this investigative department must be graduates of various levels in medical doctor, Chemistry, Law, and Computer Studies etc. But also, the graduates of the department should be tested for exams whose composition will involve the detective training academy, The Tanganyika Law Society (TLS), and Prosecution Office (DPP). This will help end an era of torment and torture to innocent people.

***

Body Searching and Inspection in Prison

It is the practice of all prisons that a prisoners or detainees must be inspected as he enters and exits the prison fort. And there is one type of search that involves stripping them naked. Rarely will the inspection be done normally without undressing. At an event of getting out of the prison building, whether you have gone to court, hospital or other prison work, it is a must to be taken to a designated area for search as well as on you return to the prison cell. The said specific area for searching has no privacy. It is an open place seen by anybody around. Entering in the ground is so shaming and insulting. If twenty or more people enter from outside, they will all be ordered to undress and squat. It is done so regardless of availability of your respectable people accompanying you. There are many who have being stripped naked before their father, son, or even father-in-law. Some detainees and prisoners were forced to close their eyes to see the nakedness of adults or respectable people inside the prison.

Apart from the search that takes place during entry and exit, there is another type of search called 'special search.' This 'special search' is done in the morning after waking up before you even get breakfast. All are placed in one area in the middle of the field and are ordered to undress, then squat and wait to be inspected one after another. The purpose of this search is to ensure that unauthorized items such as marijuana, snuff, cigarettes, alcohol, and money are not allowed to enter the prison cell.

But despite such frequent searches, these illegal items are still being incarcerated, and one of the methods used to smuggle them is called *loading*. Loading is the process of getting things into prison hidden inside the anus. It's amazing and true. I remember one morning; we were having a special search, on the field. As is the custom, for all people we were ordered to take off all our clothes and remain naked, and hold our clothes in hands. Prison officers came to search an inmate in front of me.

The prison officer said that naked person to bend down and he bent down. Banknotes were seen, as they were not loaded properly. The officer told the person to squat jump so that the notes he had loaded will get out, but it did not. This time, the Officer told him to bend again. This turn, the officer inserted his fingers into the ass of this guy without even wearing gloves. He grabbed the notes, pulled them out, and put them in his pocket. That is the search.

I am not saying that people should not be searched in prisons, but I do want them to be searched in ways that maintains dignity, humanity, and respect of human rights. Another thing is, why should prisons continue to use the same old method of stripping when this method does not solve the problem?

I was so surprised when someone passed in front of me smoking marijuana just five minutes after 'special search.' While standing in amusement, another guy came and asked me if I had extra bread for him to buy. I wondered, we have just been thoroughly searched few minutes ago where these money and marijuana comes from! I therefore concluded that searching is not that much for security effectiveness but rather humiliation and intimidations.

***

The issue of medical treatment in prison is a challenge whose solution remains a mystery. I witnessed in prison how human health was ridiculed simply because they were prisoners. I was one of the victims of that tragedy. For example, on the night of 9 November 2020, I experienced severe abdominal pain accompanied by frequent diarrhea. Early the next morning as soon as the cell door opened, I rushed to the prison clinic or sickbay as it is popularly known.

When I arrived at sickbay, I found number of patients in a queue of care and some were lying on beds waiting for treatments. Some patients were known and went to take medication according to routine, and the rest of us have not been attended by doctor. One of the things that surprised me was that the health workers at the clinic were also inmates at the prison, and there were no prison officers in charge of the exercise. I informed him of my illness to one of the service providers in the clinic, Gerald Nyandisi, who was also a Nyampara. So, I wanted to get tested and start treatment. Mr. Gerald told me that the testing is done at Mbeya Referral Hospital, as there was no testing equipments and that authorizing patients to be taken to the hospital was done only by the doctor, who was also an officer inside the prison. Unfortunately, that day he did not come to work. According to Gerald, the 'specialist' rarely visits the clinic.

I wanted to know if the doctor did not appear for a long time and how the patients at the clinic were taken care of. Mr. Gerald told me that he and two of his assistants, who are fellow inmates, were appointed by the prison administration to care for the sick. I wanted to know if the appointment was based on the qualifications and criteria of the health profession, Mr. Gerald told me that the criteria for the health profession were not considered but only discipline that gave them the opportunity to provide health services to prisoners. Gerald said, they have learned to provide health care on the sickbay, and had no previous expertise. While there waiting for the service, I saw them injecting and setting drips to some patients, I was certainly amazed at this unskilled person trying to save the lives of their peers.

I wanted to know if that day it would be possible for me to be taken to the hospital, but Mr. Gerald replied it was difficult as at the clinic there were fifteen applications from people wanting to get tested at the hospital, but the doctor has not given permission. He went on to tell me that in order to get to the hospital as soon as possible, you would probably be too sick to even walk. Mr. Gerald added that even if you are taken to hospital, there are still challenges, as you are more likely not to receive timely care, especially if your illness requires significant medical expenses. Medical services for detainees and prisoners who are hospitalized are delayed because prison authorities fail to pay for such treatment on time. Mr. Gerald gave me pills to swallow, but I expressed concern. I asked him how I could take medicine without tests. He replied that he was just using experience and may be my pain and diarrhea will go away. In other words, the guy was giving me medicine just by guessing. I certainly refused to take the pills. Later, my friend Mr. Akimu Mwakalinga gave me a natural anti-diarrheal medicine, which was leaves of trees grown at the prison mixed with ashes.

I kept searching for more information about the medical condition in the prison and came to know that most prisoners were aware of the challenge at the sickbay, so they don't bother to go there for treatments. Many of them were seeking the advice of imprisoned medical professionals who were not given the opportunity to provide care at the sickbay. There was one doctor who was a prisoner who many people followed for advice, and he was prescribing medicine, which they then imported through their relatives.

One of the people I witnessed with severe health challenges is Mr. Furaha Alick Edwin who was serving a thirty-year prison sentence. Mr. Furaha was christened 'chongo' while in prison because he has one right eye while his left eye is plucked out. 'Chongo' is a *Swahili* vocabulary that refers to a person with one eye. He lost sight in the accident while serving his sentence in a Kitai prison in Ruvuma region before being transferred to a Ruanda prison. Since then, Mr. Furaha has been accruing severe head pains. But surprisingly, he is not given any treatment. All he does is to cover himself with the fabric he made by himself.

***

How the News of President Magufuli's Death Reached Me in Prison

It was five o'clock at night on March 17, 2021. I was inside Ruanda prison in Mbeya region, cell number 16. Noises from other cells alarmed me. Considering that, noise is not allowed at night until there is a problem, as it is used as an indication that there is a problem in the relevant cell. Now, from my experience, I knew that the noise was someone being *hunted*. A week could not go by, without the incident of someone being hunted upon. 'Hunting' is prison code language means the one act of someone lying in wait for another person and raping him, especially the one sleeping next to him. The cell being overcrowded has become an opportunity for rapists to use this method to rape their colleagues in the night especially when they are lying at zero distance from each other. Do you know Prisons in Tanzania are still run by colonial laws? Imagine, in this century, prisons in Tanzania do not have telephone services. Anyway, let's get back to our topic.

But those noises shocked me because they were noises of joy to the extent, that I was shocked that there might be something different from fighting.

During that period, I had a big conflict against the prison warden officers in Mbeya Region. This came to manifest when for conference statement of the head of the Mbeya Region Prisons Officer (RPO). All these came after having raised various arguments while representing the challenges of prisoners and detainees at a meeting held in prison in front of the Commissioner General of Prisons Tanzania (CGP), the Deputy Secretary General Ministry of Internal Affairs, and MPs constituting the health committee on 6 March 2021. Due to the culture of officers, those who didn't like the challenge started torturing me by moving my cells, withholding food, and preventing my brothers and people from seeing me before being beaten by a special force called KM, as I told earlier in this chapter. I had to use the method of using the names of other detainees to enter my needs inside the prison, such as food and fruit. So those Inmates received food and fruit from my brothers and then they bring it to me.

Leaving aside the conflict with the prison officers on the other side, I was thinking of how to prepare my defense against the charges of drug trafficking after the republic closed its evidence. I had only eight days left to return to court for defense. The biggest thing is that during that period, my lawyer was unable to appear in court due to lack of travel and accommodation funds. Meanwhile, the human rights organization in Tanzania, THRDC, which provided funding to hire my lawyers, had its bank accounts closed by President Magufuli's regime.

On that day, 17 March 2021, Nyapara, Assistant Chief of the prison, was given instructions by the Prison officer on duty with the title of Inspector, instructing him to ensure that Mdude and his companions are transferred to cell number 4. This was a cell for people with mental health challenges. So, it was normal if you had a disagreement with a prison's officers; in a prison, he will transfer you to this cell as a punishment. Because life in there is tougher, threatening and so dangerous. Think of staying in the cell full of mad men. Remember that prisoners in that cell cannot sleep without applying sleeping pills, and sometimes in the middle of the night, they wake up and start causing trouble in the cell. Others relieve themselves immediately after falling asleep. This is the cell where orders were given that Mdude and his entourage should be transferred to. At the same time, you are denied the service of delivering food to the prison, your lawyer fails to come to court due to lack of accommodation funds, you are thinking of defending your case against the Republic. While you are in that situation, an order is issued to put you in a mental cell. Although I have always sacrificed my life for others, but here I needed to combine courage and madness to overcome this situation.

After those instructions, Nyapara, Assistant Chief, followed me before closing to inform me, as he was sorry to show his disagreement with his boss's instructions. I told him not to worry; I was ready to be transferred even to the toilet.

At prison's closing time, I went out carrying my bag *Shako* in my hand, which contained food, water, fruits, and clothes; I went straight to the Prison officers on duty. I asked them, "As to whether they see me as such insane to be put in the cell for people with mental health problems? That there is a cell I left home to bring here? Lock me even to the toilet, and I will sleep, but I will not stop fighting for justice." I finished that in a loud voice, my goal was to alert the detainees and the prisoners who were nearby to hear. Then, I left with a confident pace to line up in cell number 4, while some of the detainees were laughing, and others were feeling sorry for me.

It appeared that the senior duty Prison officer with the rank of ASP was not happy that I was admitted to the insane cells, even if I had a conflict with his bosses. He instructed Principal Nyapara, the assistant, to transfer me to cell number 16 from cell number 11, where I was previously staying, instead of transferring me to cell number 4 with people with mental health problems. All in all, four of my followers were sent to cell number 4.

So, I was taken to cell number 16 and we were locked up with eighty-two people, although it had the capacity to accommodate only twenty-five people. It was my habit after being locked up to take shower and then go back to my sleeping place. I did the ritual, I opened my bag, took out some food, ate and then sat leaning against the wall while reading my Bible as usual.

According to prison procedures, at nine o'clock in the night, it is time to listen to the news from various radio stations. After the news report, the order is given by the duty Nyapara in the cell to turn off the radio until the morning, to listen to the BBC Swahili news report.

Until the cell radio is turned off at ten o'clock at night, there was no new news other than the news we hear every day. So, we went to sleep. Now, there are people who have their own radio. So, when the command to turn off the radio is given, they continue to listen to the radio in a very low volume so that it is difficult to detect them. Well, these are the ones who heard Vice President Samia Suluhu announcing the death of President Magufuli around eleven o'clock at night.

Remember, Magufuli's regime, he once ordered prisoners to be kicked and to work continuously. Also, on the side of the detainees, there was a cry of being stuck with the case and then the cases of economic and the investigation did not take place for years and years. So, neither the prisoners nor the detainees enjoyed the rule of President Magufuli. Now when I listen carefully to the noises from the neighboring cell, I heard one of them saying, "God has heard our cry this man said that we should be kicked and worked continuously."

That's when I learned that President Magufuli has passed away, considering that, there were rumors of his illness in recent days. I told the people of our cell to turn on the radio if there is news of the death of President Magufuli. It is true that they turned on the radio and I heard Vice President Samia Suluhu announcing the national tragedy. Inside the cell now, people cheered and followed me, while I was sleeping and lifted me up until they hurt my leg. But I didn't even see it as a problem for me despite the fact that I suffered from the pain for several weeks.

The death of President Magufuli taught me that when you have power, it is important to avoid torturing and hurting other people. For us Christians, JESUS instructed us not to do to others what we do not want to be done to us. Therefore, if you are a Christian and then you use your power to treat others, as you do not want to be treated, even if we pray for your grave a thousand times, it is in vain before Almighty God.

***

Homosexuality in Prison

Prisons in Tanzania are populated by people of different religions. There are Muslims and Christians in large numbers, who are always conducting prayers to God throughout the day. People of different tribes and even nationalities conduct intensive prayers in the prison, often using their own language. For instance, you may find Ethiopian citizens, who are mostly imprisoned for illegal immigration, standing against prison wall, singing and praying loudly by their Ethiopian language. I have had witnessed a man who was facing murder charges who, every morning after being released from our cells, would go straight to the place of worship, kneel down, and start worshiping for about four hours non-stop. There was a day when a man prayed for about seven hours without resting or eating anything until I had to approach him in his place of worship. I witnessed the man praying to God with mucus and tears running down to his shirt. I was even more surprised a week later when he was acquitted and released on *Nolle Prosequi*. That's when I believed that there are also true and strong believers even in prisons.

At first, when talked about homosexuality in prisons, I thought it was just mere stories. I believed that prison is hell on earth and that it was home of infallible persons. I believed that most of the prisoners and detainees in prison are strongly stressed by the charges facing them as well as their prison terms. I knew they spend a lot of time worshiping God so that he may ease the burden of their prison pains. This came to be proved wrong in my stay in the prison

One day, in the middle of the night, a loud shout was heard in our cell (in the *Census* area); "I have already caught the evidence." The words were clearly spoken by a helpless man. The whole cell was shocked considering that noise is not allowed at night. Nyapala's of the cell and I got up and moved to the scene. I was stunned after seeing one of the prisoners holding tightly the penis of a fellow prisoner, which was near his hips while he kept saying, "I already have the evidence he wanted to rape me." The accused prisoner, whose penis had been grabbed by force after an attempted rape was crying while defending himself that he was looking for a book. When asked by Nyapara that since when he started 'looking for books at night on people's hips using his penis,' he failed to answer. He continued to cry while defending himself and asked to have his penis be released as it have been pulled by the victim of rape attempt. Later, the rapist was given a punishment of fifteen *Mbata's,* as the prison rules dictate, and then he was put sleep in the toilet.

That incident surprised me a lot considering the harsh conditions in our prisons, from the standard of food to accommodation and treatment etc. My mind was so astonished as to how is it possible that besides all those troubles in the prison still someone will have enough courage to rape his fellow man? This is so unbecoming.

Another day, early in the morning; I was surprised to see one of the prisoners on the roof of the prison kitchen holding two knives. It is unknown where he got them, as knives or anything harmful are not allowed to be brought into the prison. The prisoner was shouting that he did not agree with the order to transfer him to prison and leave his gay lover behind. The prisoner had been ordered to be transferred from the Ruanda prison in Mbeya to the agricultural prison in Rukwa region. The prisoner claimed that he was ready to die but could never accept being transferred to another prison and leave his lover to be inherited by other people who were stalking him in the prison. I was more surprised when he praised his gay who is a fellow man that he has an attractive neck like a giraffe while the detainees burst out laughing. Later, he was forcibly taken down by prison officers, and unfortunately, one of the two knives he was holding injured himself in his hand. He was then transported to the prison where he was sentenced to be deported to.

The other day in the cell, I saw one of the Nyaparas helping a young prisoner drink tea as if he was attending to a patient. Then the Nyapara went to the bathroom, and prepared water for the boy to bathe, and stood at the door to protect the boy while he was taking a bath.

I asked if the young man is sick and if the Nyapara had offered to help him. I was told that the young man is not sick but has been persuaded by the Nyapara to agree to be gay so that the Nyapara would help him not to suffer in prison. I continued to be told that the Nyapara is weeding love for the young man who turned his wife. The fact that even the Nyapara guards the door while the young man is taking a shower is due to jealousy of love and he is afraid of other same-homosexual partners stealing the young man. I was stunned and even more surprised when I was told that there is a time when the Nyapara cleans him to remove the remains of the boy's feces after defecating. Indeed, the world has wonders.

During the four hundred and fourteen days I spent in prison, I researched these acts of Homosexuality and rape. One of the main reasons that led to these actions is the lack of the right to marriage for prisoners and inmates in prison. That according to the laws of Tanzania, not having sex with your wife or husband while in prison is part of the punishment for prisoners and detainees.

That the wife, husband, or lover is allowed to visit you in prison but is not allowed attending the marriage ceremony. 'Tanzanian laws do not allow prisoners and detainees to have a marriage ceremony in prison.'

This reason leads some of them to start desiring their fellow men as a substitute for their lovers or wives. I say that is the main reason because most of them I interviewed had never done these acts before entering the prison. Most of the men who are gay in prison have never been gay before imprisonment. Again, those few who desires to live without being disturbed, tortured and eating good food is what has made many young people gay. Most of the victims are young men under the age of twenty-five and Ethiopians who are the many in Tanzanian prisons and most of them are arrested for illegal immigration. According to the statistics of 2021, Tanzanian prisons had 1789 Ethiopian prisoners. This is according to the information provided on the *Jamii Forums* page quoting President Magufuli at the event to welcome the President of Ethiopia in January 2021. Some of them have contracted *HIV* and other sexually transmitted diseases while in prison. Imagine a person entered prison with good health and then comes out with *HIV* that he got from being converted to a wife in prison; how painful is that?

When young men are brought to the prison cell, homosexuals are astounded and excited, you may think they have seen Miss World. Many of them start setting traps for these young men to trap them and turn them into gays. Traps can be to torture them and then they appear to help them or give them good food and give them chance to sleep at the *VIP* space. All of these are methods of ensnaring young people. And many who use these methods are those prisoners and detainees with positions in the prison, including the Nyapara. Imagine a man who can set traps to persuade his fellow man to accept being gay and then turn him into his wife. I knew I had finished seeing the wonders of the world, but I still haven't. When they manage to catch one, they do their love secretly so that they are not known because the punishment is severe, including being stripped of the titles they have in the prison. They will also be beaten and locked in the punishment rooms for seven days. For those who are weak and do not have any positions to enable them catch gays, they often have to rape people who are sleeping next to them, taking advantage of the opportunity to squeeze, especially for those who are sleeping in the 'Census.'

Many men who do such acts to their partners have spent a long time in prison. And some of them went to prison when they were young, and they were treated like that and now they follow the same culture of doing it to others. Very few young people started homosexuality before entering prison, but most of them started while in prison.

***

My Advice to the Government

Due to this situation, I'm advising the government of Tanzania to start giving right to prisoners and detainees to enjoy sexual right with their partners when they are visited in prison. Being a prisoner does not deprive one of this basic human rights. This will help to reduce or completely stop the acts of rape in prisons.

If the government agrees to grant the marriage rights of marriage to prisoners when visited by their partners, then it should make improvements to the buildings by creating special rooms in prisons for that purpose.

That there are special cells for young people under the age of twenty-five and foreign nationals to save them from falling into the danger of being turned into the 'wives' of lustful prisoners.

All cases should be bailable to reduce the crowding, which is proved to be a reason for people to sleep tight and lead to acts of rape in the cell at midnight. According to the news published on 10 February 2020 by the Swahili DW channel from Germany, it was made clear that 56.7 percent of the people in prison are detainees. In a simple sense, there are more detainees in our prisons than prisoners. This overcrowding of the prison by detainees is due to many of criminal offenses not being bailable. Therefore, I advise the government to start a legal process that will enable all cases to have bail in order to reduce the number of people in prisons.

If the Tanzanian government takes this advice into account, *HIV* infection and other sexually transmitted diseases will also decrease.

VII
JUDGEMENT

"It is better to release a guilty suspect than to imprison an innocent one."
— Barnabas A. Samatta

It was on 9 December 2020, the nation was celebrating fifty-ninth years of Tanganyika's independence. That day I was conducting physical practices in the Ruanda prison where I had been detained since 13 May 2020. It was my custom to do regular physical exercises throughout my time in prison. As I continued to practice, I kept thinking in my head that it was now fifty-nine years since our country gained independence. I kept wondering what that freedom would mean if among the citizens were in prison for political cases? What will that freedom mean if opponents' arguments are answered by gunshots? What does that freedom mean if there is no right to comment, the right to assemble, the right to vote, and to be elected? After these questions, I answered myself that the celebrated freedom is the freedom of the rulers and not the freedom of the people.

After my practices, I returned to rest under a shadow of the tree at my tent, or 'mesi' in prison language. Seating chairs are lined plastic buckets that our relatives have brought to us in the prison. These buckets are used in storing dishes, washing, put in the utensils, and store the foodstuffs that our relatives might bring to us. But since there are no chairs in the prison, the buckets are turned into chairs. While I was resting there a friend of mine, whom I met in prison, Vuyo Jack, joined me. Mr. Vuyo is a South African citizen and was serving a twenty-five-year sentence imprison. He informed me that on the eve of that day he had a dream that was about him and me. One of the things I learnt in prison was that dreams are more important than anything else. A person who dreams of being in prison in the morning wanders to the clergy inside the prison to find the interpretation of his dream. I later learnt that a large percentage of those dreams comes true, and that is why people pay attention to them.

Mr. Vuyo told me about his dream that he saw me and him sitting at the same area under a tree inside the prison. He says we were amazed at the passenger plane that was flying over the prison. Suddenly, that large Boeing Dreamliner passed by, and while we were watching it and to our surprise it crashed on the prison ground. Mr. Vuyo says after the plane crashed, People wearing military uniforms entered the prison and took me, Mdude, in custody, accusing me of being involved in the downing the plane. Vuyo says he and other people inside the prison defended me that I was not responsible for the crashing of the plane, as prisoners are not allowed to enter with any dangerous objects, let alone firearms. The men then argued and agreed that I was not responsible for the plane crash. They opened the prison gates and set me free.

Mr. Vuyo says after my release he felt lonely and he went to the prison TV to watch news. As he sat watching the news report, he saw Tanzanian Vice President Samia Suluhu Hassan issuing a presidential pardon for many prisoners and Mr. Vuyo was one of the people who did not benefit from it. The tale of Vuyo's dream ended.

Mr. Vuyo told me after the dream he felt happy, as he believed on that day, he would receive a pardon from the President as is the custom for him to grant presidential pardon to prisoners on 9 December and 26 April of every year. He also believed that through his dream, President Magufuli would order the DPP to drop the charges and I would be released.

Later, a bell rang to indicate something was wrong. So, prisoners and detainees gathered at the arena to wait for calls or orders. Ten minutes later, the prison warden and his officers arrived and began announcing the names of the prisoners who had been pardoned by the President. Mr. Vuyo was not one of the prisoners pardoned.

After the warden finished announcing the names, we were allowed to disperse and returned to the 'mesi.' As we sat down, I told Mr. Vuyo, "Your dream was false because according to our Tanzanian constitution, the President alone has the power to pardon prisoners and not the vice president as you dreamt. Also, President Magufuli cannot order the DPP to drop charges against me."

Vuyo laughed a little and then insisted that this could happen as he prayed for seven days, so he believes God showed him the way through a dream and that only patience is needed. I went on denying Mr. Vuyo's dream as it was unconstitutional. Next to us sat another friend of mine named Mbaruku Khamis. The friend told Mr. Vuyo to just calm down because dreams and reality are two different things. He told Mr. Vuyo in a joke that, "Mdude is only arguing with experience and that is why, due to his controversy the government have failed to combat him and decided to bring him to prison. Now, will you be able to win arguments against him?" We laughed happily and then changed the story and waited for three o'clock in the afternoon to be locked up in our cells like a native cow being brought back to the booth after being headed from the pasture.

On 17 March 2021, the death of President John Pombe Magufuli was announced, and on 19 March 2021, Vice President Samia Suluhu Hassan was sworn in as President of the United Republic of Tanzania. On 26 April 2021, President Samia pardoned five-thousand prisoners and Mr. Vuyo Jack was among those who benefitted. He had five years cut from his sentence. Mr. Vuyo followed me in a happy mood and asked me, "Mdude are you still arguing about my 9 December 2020 dream?" I remained silent and kept glancing at him with smile.

From that day, I began to believe that I would win the case and be acquitted by the court. That is why I kept urging all those who attended the court to follow up with my case that they should no worry, as I will one day win the case and be released from prison.

***

Finally, on 28 June 2021, I was brought out to the court from prison with handcuffs on my hands. Relatives and supporters of CHADEMA flooded the courtroom, and others couldn't get seats and had to wait outside the court building. After a while, senior resident magistrate Hon. Z. D. Laizer entered the courtroom to read the sentence.

State Attorney Mr. Davice stood up and introduced the other state attorneys as well as the defense Advocates Mr. Faraji Mangula and Mr. Swedi Shilinde. The state attorney informed the court that I, the suspect, was also present in person.

Both parties stated that they were ready for judgement.

The magistrate began giving a brief history of the case by identifying the accused person against the Republic as *Mdude Mpaluka Nyagali*. The case was brought before this court on 27 May 2020 on suspicion of drug trafficking in contravention of section 15A (1) of the Drug Control and Anti-Drugs Act no. 5 of 2015 and its amendments. In this case, the defendant is accused of trafficking Heroine Hydrochloride drug weighing 23.4 grams.

In the indictment, the accused was arrested, and later subjected to a search where he was found with the same number of drugs in his residence in Itezi area in Mbeya City. The search was conducted by the police force under ASP Siame, an assistant to RCO Mbeya, on 11 May 2020. The specimens of the suspected drug were sent to a state chemist and completed an examination confirming that they were heroin Hydrochloride. This investigative exercise was completed on 12 May 2021 under a state chemist who testified before this court as witness no. 1 of the republic.

The magistrate went on to read the sentence. In witness statement No. 2 of the republic, the accused was arrested after posting on social media false information and incitement against the former President of the United Republic of Tanzania, Late Dr. John Pombe Magufuli. The statement, which was not released in court, aimed at tarnishing the image of the ruling CCM government.

The accused was arrested on 10 May 2020 in CHADEMA office in the areas known as Kadege with a colleague named Fadhili Shombe. They were taken to the RCO office where he was ordered to hand over his phone and home and office keys. ASP Siame took him to the office of Inspector Joram for questioning, but the defendant refused to provide the information in the absence of his lawyer. So, the accused had to be taken into custody at the Central Police Station where he slept until the next day.

On the next day, a man who identified himself as Fadhili Shombe came to the office of the RCO and introduced himself as the personal counsel of the defendant, stating that he wanted to see his client. Fadhili was taken to where the accused was, and the defendant agreed to co-operate in the exercise of writing question statement. But, before writing the statement, ASP Siame ordered them to first go to the defendant's residence to conduct a search.

That, the journey to the defendant's home began with a police car carrying officers ASP Siame, who is a Witness PW2, Cpl Charles, who is a PW6 witness here in the court, the defendant himself, and Fadhili, the defendant's lawyer.

The magistrate went on to read the sentence that; when they arrived at the home of the accused, a man named John Rasek Manyumba, who here in court has been a witness for the republic number PW8, was called by phone to be a free witness in the search. The accused was shocked to find that there was also another police vehicle at his home, which was loaded with heavily armed police officers. Before the defendant was ordered to open the door, he was told that he had the right to search the officers who came for the search. After searching ASP Siame, Cpl Charles, and three other fellow officers, they entered and began a search. They started a search in his bedroom, picking up one small phone. They went on to the guest room, and found another phone, and seized it as well. They continued searching the closet and finally to the living room, where they took twenty-four CDs. At the end of the search, one of them picked up a khaki envelope with nylon bags in it. The object found was suspected to be drugs.

Continuing to read the verdict, the magistrate said the accused had doubted that the search had the following flaws:
- He searched only three officers. But there were at least ten officers at the scene.
- The keys to his house were in the hands of police officers from the day he was arrested until they came to hand them to him when they arrived at his house during a search.
- When he asked why he did not search all those who were present at his residence during the search, he was told that the officers were there for security reasons.
- The defendant strongly opposed the summoning of a CCM leader who is not recognized by law in witnessing legal searches. What he does know is that the person with that legal authority is the local chairman. The presence of the CCM cadre and the accused being the CHADEMA cadre was a serious flaw.
- At the time of the search, whilst in the living room door was not locked from inside as required by law. And when the defendant questioned why they should not close the door first, he was told that there was nothing wrong with leaving it open.
- While searching his room, one of the soldiers suddenly left and returned to the room five minutes later. Defendant asked him where he had gone, but the officer had no better answers but to ask him to be at peace.

The magistrate went on to say that; Exhibits seized during the search were handed over to the police and handed over to Cpl Ally, who in this court is witness number PW3, for safekeeping. The next day the exhibits were filed in front of the accused and an independent witness identified as Semeni Ally, who is witness number PW4, and was forwarded to the state chemist.

At the hearing of this case, the prosecution was represented by the State Attorney; Mr. Siraji Iboru, Mr. Hebe Kihaka, and Mr. Davice Msanga. The defense was represented by Advocate Faraji Mangula.

The magistrate went on to read the verdict that the prosecution brought to court a total of eight witnesses and fourteen exhibits, while the defense presented only one witness and three exhibits.

Prosecution witnesses were PW1 – Jansen Bilaro (Government chemist), PW2 – ASP Sylvester Clement Siame, PW3 – D / Cpl Ally, PW4 – Semeni Ally Mkina, PW5 – Audifas Pilato Silayo, PW6 – D / Cpl Charles, PW7 – Peter Bwetela, and PW8 – John Manyumba.

The witness in the defense was Mr. Mdude Mpaluka Nyagali.

The magistrate continued reading the verdict and that the first witness confirmed to the court that he had examined the samples brought to the laboratory and found that it was a heroine drug weighing 23.4 grams. He explained that the drugs are dangerous to the health of the user. The Witness explained the laboratory procedure he followed in examining the specimen, how he came to find the result, and finally how he wrote a report for the entire diagnostic exercise.

That; Second witness, ASP Siame, told the court how he led the squad to arrest Mdude on suspicion of writing obscene and false words against the late government of Dr. John Magufuli. He described how they arrested him and remanded him in custody. The witness went on to describe how he conducted a search operation at the defendant's home and the outcome of the search, as described in the preliminary stages of this sentence. The witness went on to tell the court how the exhibits found in the defendant's home were detained, kept, and eventually sent to a state chemist. Other information of the witness includes the results of the investigation, the manner in which the handover of the exhibits and the information was made and the opening of this case against the defendant.

The third witness for the prosecution is G2513 D / Cpl Ally. DC Ally explained how the specimens that were feared to be drugs were handed to him and that he also participated in the sealing exercise with the aim of taking them to a state chemist for investigation. The witness testified in court that the exhibits were sealed in front of the accused by an independent witness who was identified as Semeni.

The fourth witness, Ms. Semeni Ally Mkina, who is a food vendor, testified in the court that she was present to witness the sealing of the exhibits.

The fifth witness is Mr. Audifas Pilate Silayo, who identified himself in court as the owner of the house where the accused lived. He said that he personally did not know Mdude Mpaluka But had been seeing his name as a tenant on the tenant agreement. He never had a quarrel with him over paying rent.

The sixth witness is Cpl Charles. He testified in court that he had participated in the search and that among the items they found in the defendant's home were items in nylon bags containing powder that were feared to be drugs. The items were inside a khaki envelope. The witness provided the court with information on how the search was conducted, and how the items were found, how they were sent to be stored, examined, and the results of the government chemist's laboratory examination.

The seventh Witness, Mr. Peter Bwetele, introduced himself as the caretaker of the house where the accused lived. He manages the house on behalf of the landlord, Mr. Audifas Pilato Silayo – PW5. The defendant, as a tenant, has been entering into an agreement with me. He pays the money to Mr. Bwetele, and then he sends the money to the landlord. Bw. Bwetele says that Mr. Mdude has no problem paying for the rent and is a very friendly person with his fellow tenants.

The judge went on to read the sentence that; The eighth witness, Mr. John Manyumba, a member of the ten houses in the area where the accused lived, told the court how he had been called by telephone and that he had come to witness a search operation in the house where the accused lived. He told the court that he was not a government official but a member of his CCM party. He also told the court that he did not know the accused by official identity, as when he moved to his street, he did not go to identify himself to him. He only knows him as a neighbor and not on official basis.

After the presentation of the evidence by these prosecution witnesses, led by state attorneys and interrogated by the defense counsel, then the prosecution closed their case.

The magistrate went on to say that, it was time for the defense, where the defense counsel led the only witness in this case Mr. Mdude Mpaluka Nyagali to tell the court the truth about the charges in court.

The magistrate went on reading the verdict and said the witness who was the accused began by telling the court that all charges against him were false and that they were fabricated due to hostility between him and the police force in the country. The witness told the court that he had been severely tortured by the Police Force. He has been abducted several times by the police force; he was severely tortured from 2016 to 2019. He explained that due to the severe torture he received from the police force and the hostility between him and the police force, he decided to file a lawsuit against the IGP, Attorney General, RPC for Songwe, and other police officers. The witness also told the court that he had sent a letter of complaint against the police brutality to the Commission on Human Rights and Good Governance. "My actions have led me to be hunted by the police force all the time. These charges are only part of what I am being subjected to by the police force. They have made this case with the intention of completely extinguishing me."

The witness told the court about how he was arrested along with a colleague whom he identified as Fadhili Shombe. When they were brought to the RCO's office in Mbeya, Shombe was evicted and was not allowed to receive the accused's phone and keys, as was a plea from the accused to the police.

The magistrate went on saying that the defendant explained to the court how the search was conducted at his residence on 11 May 2020. He described all the steps they went through and what he saw as flaws in the search operation. For example, the search was full of violations of search rules and regulations where even a search warrant was not issued. Above all, some of the specimens seized in the search, such as the khaki envelope, which was said to contain five bags of drugs, had never been brought to court. The defendant explained how the absence of the khaki envelope could affect the course of justice. Defendant strongly objected to the presence of a cadre of the ruling Party—CCM in the search instead of the local government chairman elected by popular vote and who is legally recognized to have the authority to witness the search in his constituency.

The magistrate went on reading the sentence that the court found that the charges against the accused were flawed, provided that the evidence presented in court was incomplete. The prosecution has failed to prove and convince the court that they had convincing evidence that leaves no doubt to convict the defendant. Defects of the witnesses' statements regarding the handover of exhibits among witnesses brought to court indicated that there was no truth in the charges against the accused. And last but not least, the illegal system of relying on state-of-the-art electronic chemist information.

The magistrate said she had also reviewed the final summary documents of the lawyers on both sides and commended them for the good work they had done including the good return of the court functions.

The magistrate said she had thoroughly reviewed the evidence presented in court by the review of lawyers for both sides of the case. The point in this case is whether the prosecution has proved beyond a reasonable doubt that the defendant is guilty.

Then she said that the court had received evidence information that had been presented and that was not disputed between the two parties. Similarly, in what the prosecution accused the defendant, the court has gone through to prove that all the evidences and exhibits presented in court intended to make the court satisfied that the allegations against the accused are true.

According to the evidences presented in the court, it is the second witness who testified that it is true that the accused was arrested on charges of writing and posting false information and misrepresentation against the late John Pombe Magufuli government. The accused was arrested, detained, searched, and later prosecuted.

The magistrate went on to read the sentence that the court found that there were matters, which in the manner presented by the prosecution witnesses made the court feel that the prosecution had failed to prove beyond a reasonable doubt the allegations against the accused.

The magistrate says, for example, according to the second and sixth witnesses, it is true that in the residence of the accused during the search there were several other unidentified soldiers except for the second witness who was the leader of the search operation. The court finds that this presence in the search area of many unidentified police officers makes the evidence against the defendant unable to substantiate the allegations against him.

Although the evidence presented here is that the accused opened the door to his home, there is a fact that the keys were in the hands of police officers from the day he was arrested.

The magistrate said the court also considered suspicions of the police's insistence on summoning a member of the ten houses instead of the local chairperson to witness the search operation. Even the envoy admitted in court that he did not know the accused, as he had never been to his office to identify himself when he moved to the area. The search was, therefore, carried out without the presence of an independent witness. This feature automatically defects when a search is complete. Consider the case between Togora Wambura versus the Director of Public Prosecutions, Appeal Case No. 212. This search also lacks status due to the lack of *'Search warrant'* from the police force.

The magistrate continued stating that the case was based on a search conducted at the defendant's home. The lack of legitimacy of the search due to defects found in it makes the prosecution unable to prove in any way that the accused is guilty.

The magistrate went on to say that, the defendant told the court and testified that he was in a very bad relationship with the police force. In a feud between the police and the accused, the police have been severely torturing the suspect they have repeatedly arrested, abducted, and tortured him severely. The defendant told the court that he had filed charges against the IGP, AG, and several police officers in the High Court Mbeya Zone. He has also written a letter to the Commission on Human Rights and Good Governance complaining against the IGP and the entire police force for acts of violation of human rights and humiliating treatments by the force. The magistrate added that the court had received several exhibits from the accused, which showed the court that there was a lot of enmity between the accused and the police force.

The defense from the accused proves to the court that there are many doubts that the case against him has been fabricated and that there is not enough evidence from the prosecution to substantiate the allegations made in court against the accused. The prosecution has therefore failed to prove beyond a reasonable doubt that the defendant is guilty. This court has therefore found the defendant not guilty and dismisses the charges against him for drug possession in contravention of section 15 (1) (a) of the Anti-Drug Control Act Chapter 95 amended 2019.

That is how the magistrate ended reading the sentence.

After that sentence, I was certainly overjoyed. Although I was confident that I would win, but I did not believe what happened. The first thing I did before I talked to anyone was, I closed my eyes and said a prayer of thanks to God.

I remembered in the Holy Bible the letter of the Apostle Peter to the chosen who went to teach the word of God in foreign places in Pontus, Galatia, Cappadocia, Bithynia, and Asia. In that letter, the Apostle Peter told them that, *for this is thankworthy, if a man for conscience toward God endure grief, suffering wrongfully.* – 1 Peter 2:19

Hundreds of people in the courtroom were overjoyed and some shed tears. Through the media and social media, I saw many Tanzanians, regardless of their political and religious differences, rejoicing over my release.

VIII
ALUTA CONTINUA

We start and end with GOD.

Many people believe that if it were not for the death of President Magufuli, today I, Mdude, would be a prisoner in one of the prisons in Tanzania. Even I myself believe so. The drug case against me could have made me end in prison for up to thirty years or life imprisonment, by the order from above, which President Magufuli actually instituted, had been issued and followed. But there is a God who is supreme and who subdues the plans of men and then enforces His wills, and there is no one to oppose him.

It is God, who gives me the courage to publicly defend human rights and condemn acts of human rights abuses, knowing that the authorities hate that confidence. It was God, who saved me from death when the kidnappers and persecutors attempted to kill me. That is the God with whom we, the advocates of justice, begin and end with.

There are many Tanzanians, who have been killed by some officers of the security forces who have given themselves or are given the task of silencing President Magufuli's opponents. There are also those who have escaped from the hand of death like me but do not want to say, I believe one day God will force them to speak. They will say all that they have experienced and expose the evils of President Magufuli and his cronies. Then, those who see him as a hero and the pious, who do not understand this simple truth that at his presence I would have ended gaining thirty years or life imprisonment will be forced to understand. Although I believe, there are some of us, who do not want to see his animosity regardless of heap of evidences given to them but the truth will stand. God is always the master of truth

There are others, who claim that the persecution against me was due to the extremism in politics. And that I was using harsh words in my criticism against President Magufuli. They went as far as advising me to use soft language that would not offend President Magufuli just like many other criticizers of Magufuli's government used to do. According to them, this would have minimized reasons for me to be persecuted. The question is which criticizer of President Magufuli have never been persecuted? There is none. All that criticized him have suffered in one way or another.

There were many others who really liked my position. They comforted me when I faced problems due to my political stretch and then encouraged me to never surrender. There were former Magufuli supporters who hated me, and others expressed their feelings publicly that I was supposed to be jailed or I should not continue living on the grounds that I was using abusive language against President Magufuli even though no court has ever found me guilty of any of the allegations I was accused of from time to time. There are others, who also advise me to stop these movements to escape from more sufferings and instead use that time to raise money for the family and me. The answer is this 'planning is choosing', I chose to defend the voiceless people in our nation. I am willing to endure in suffering and waste my valuable time for the benefit of my society. I am called by GOD to defend justice, righteousness, and equality.

Perhaps my patriotism and courage accompanied by feelings of suffering while demanding justice and equality in our nation is what makes some people interpret it as a use of strong language. But also, those people should know that; the truth hurts and no soft language will make the hungry Lion invading your herd to be scared and run away. The movement for justice and equality in any nation is like the gospel, and there is no gospel with soft words. I am not sure if there is any nation in the world whose people gained justice and freedom through soft words.

With great boldness, I move forward in the struggle for justice and condemning against evils. I will also continue to promote good governance and the rule of law in the wider interests of Tanzanian society. I did and will continue to do this with great boldness and plenty of passion.

Although police force refuted my social accounts, this did not and will not reduce my urge to fight for justice and equality.

There are a number of things that have been strengthening me from my imprisonment to my release. One is the support I received from my CHADEMA party along with activists, institutions and other well-wishers. The party assisted me by giving me an advocate who defended me from the beginning to the end. The THRDC and the LHRC assisted the lawyers who assisted the party counsel, not forgetting philanthropical support and contributions made by CHADEMA members to assist me throughout my life in prison. Crowds of CHADEMA members and leaders were attending my case whenever it was heard. Although I was incarcerated in the worst-case scandal, I found peace of mind to have seen Chairman Freeman Mbowe attending my trial.

It is very encouraging. This solidarity is a sign that there is a large group of people in the community who are committed to fighting for justice in our country. Another thing is how the local and foreign media were reporting to the world about incidents of abduction and torture of which I am a victim and one of the witnesses. The noise of media outlets such as BBC, DW Kiswahili, VOA Swahili and the noise of activists using social media terrified the kidnappers and persecutors thus made them fail to kill me. Without these noises, I would probably have died.

Being reported on the media frequently, especially through social media made me so popular that for instance when I arrived at the Oysterbay in 2016 an inmate recognized me and released information to the CHADEMA members. Had I not been famous I would probably not have been identified and therefore, information of my being detained in Dar es Salaam would not have leaked. That would have given the kidnappers a chance to torture and even kill me. I remember one kidnapper, in May 2019, claiming that even if people shouted, they could still kill me, then sit down with the ambassadors representing donor countries, and end the existing anguish from them and citizens. Although, I could not look at him in the eyes due to me being blindfolded, I did know that the torturer had a psychological crisis due to the online noise about my abduction. Most of the abducted ones had no person to talk for them and so they 'disappeared' silently. By the same token, cyber heroes and protesters combating human rights abuses should increase as much as possible.

I want the noise to increase because our country is already invaded by cruel, disloyal, and shameless people within the security forces. Heads of state agencies, for example, the police force, have been publicly denouncing their brutality. One example is former Dodoma regional police commander, Gilles Muroto. He threatened citizens who wanted to protest against the 2019, local government election rigging, saying they would be beaten like dogs. Muroto did not stop there, but went further and said that government opponents had been beaten by voters with a 'toothless dog' at the ballot box, and that Dodoma police will extremely beat whoever opposing this victory.

Muroto concluded his remarks as 'those are their greetings,' another is Mr. Jonathan Shana, who was the Regional Police Commander of the Arusha. He identified himself as a CCM member by publicly announcing that the police force as a state body is under the control of the government, and the government belongs to CCM, and therefore the state organs belong to CCM. Mr. Muroto is currently retired while Mr. Shana is deceased. There are many other examples of officials, of the state, who publicly identified themselves as advocates and defenders of the ruling party and strongly undermine the opposition. Everyone who follows Tanzanian politics is a witness to this fact. That is why; I insist that whistleblowers are needed as much as possible.

***

President Magufuli's dictatorial regime produced many dictators among our Tanzanian society. A nation may have a lot of bad-minded people, but they will not be seen until a bigger bad-minded national leader like them emerges, and then they will start to show up in large numbers. These dictators included some of officials in the security forces who used their position to hurt the opposition practitioners challenging the government. These criminal servants of the nation did these things by using their public offices contrary to the laws of the land. They sometimes did that without instructions but only for their selfish gains. For example, RCO Katimbo of Mbeya region made it clear to me that he is taken from very far by IGP Simon Sirro and therefore he would not allow his boss to be played upon. By that time, I had filed a lawsuit against the police force.

Ole Sabaya, Henry James, Paul Makonda, Ali Hapi, Kenani Kihongosi, Simon Odunga are just few mentioned of the many young people who demonstrated their dictatorship when they were given leadership positions in the dictatorship regime of John Magufuli. Their stories are on the records of the media and social networks. They preached hatred, practiced persecution and even murder against political opponents.

Furthermore, some of them have not ended up speaking on stages but also actively participated in the abduction, torture and killed many young Tanzanians who dared to challenge them and or President Magufuli. A good example of these young people is Ole Sabaya, a former Hai District Commissioner, who is serving a thirty-year sentence for armed robbery w before appealing that freed him. However, the state prosecutor's office has removed the other charges against him and he is now free. He also has allegations of kidnapping and torturing people that have not been officially reported to law enforcement agencies.

Some dictators did not have titles, but they sought prominence by showing their dictatorship in order to win the heart of John Magufuli, who was keen to nominate young people with dictatorial traits like his own. Cyprian Musiba was a good example in this category. He used the shadow of free activism to spread hatred against Magufuli's opponents while writing scandals through his newspapers. Musiba once dared to say that no court in Tanzania could convict him. He gave reasons for saying this by claiming that all courts are under Magufuli. What a dictatorship!

But there are also those who have given themselves the task of intimidating government criticizers through messages, which they posted on social media. They either published the threats publicly or sent them to their alleged victims. An example of people in this category is a man named Nick Mikely. I remember that fourteen days before I was arrested and charged with drug trafficking, I received heavy threats on my Instagram page from a man who called himself Nick Mikely. The man threatened me with a short message he sent in response to my text. He clearly said that this time I will be lost and there would never be any mistakes made as was done in the former abductions. The message pondered my heart so much, so I decided to track down this person. I wanted to find out who he was and where does he get the courage to intimidate me.

After an investigation, I found out that Mr. Nick Mikely was a Soldier of the Anti-Drug Squad and his office was in Dar es Salaam. But Mr. Nick Mikely, as he calls himself on Instagram, was among the United Nations Soldiers – African Mission in Darful – UNAMID. I noticed this through one of her photos wearing a UNAMID shirt, all these small but notorious dictators calmed down as does the ice melts in the hot sun after the death of President Magufuli. They are cowards. People who do not like to hear different opinions but opt to take negative steps to hurt others are cowards and mentally weak. When they lose power as they did after Magufuli's death, they become as small as chaff.

***

Social media has become a major force in contributing to political decision-making in Tanzania, as I mentioned earlier. During John Magufuli's dictatorial regime, the government fought social media but it was then that they gained more power. President Magufuli himself was once quoted as saying he wished the angels would come down and shut down social media. Unfortunately, he did not live to see that happen if at all it could happen. For their part, the activists devised more methods of self-defense and information was spreading rapidly. The most popular and widely circulated reports and messages are those of anti-government, as well as those pertaining to the activities of activists and opposition politicians. Sometimes truth and falsehood were mixed and people did not care about. They carried it as it was.

For example, after I was arrested and charged with drug trafficking, there were rumors circulating on social media that a woman who was allegedly a member of the national security department was the one who put drugs in my residence. The fabricated reports claimed that the woman was my girlfriend and was sending me money. They continued propagating that the woman came to my house and stayed for several days. After completing her drug plan, she said goodbye and left before the police came to my house and find the drugs.

These statements are not true. If the plan to use a woman existed, then the police would not have bothered to call some CHADEMA members to ask for my phone number and places where I live. Also, if there was a woman's plan to put drugs at my residence, then the police would not bother to arrest and detain me for incitement charges and go to search my home on the following day. Another question is as to why the police confiscated my house keys before going to search? Wouldn't that allegation be stronger if I was left with the keys and an alleged woman has left drugs in my home?

Why did they now snatch the keys from me when the woman has already planted drugs exhibit in my home? The answer is that no woman was sent to put drugs in my house, neither did any woman visited me at my home before being arrested by the police. It is a big lie spread digitally. The truth is that the police arrested me when I left the CHADEMA office. They took the keys to my house because they wanted to go to my house to put drugs while I was in custody. When they interrogated me, the police asked me if I lived with my family or anyone else and I replied that I was living on my own. I think that was the mistake I made, and they took advantage of the situation to set drug trap in my home. Now, I do not know what the motives of those who fabricated such propaganda were.

***

Aluta Continua! The struggle continues. The struggle I am witnessing in our country, and which I am participating in, is a struggle between defenders of justice and oppressors. The struggle between true believers of truth and the liars. It is more than a struggle for those who want to gain political authority and those who have it. Although those in power have often used force and brutal means to fight the powerless, the scales seem to be leaning towards the powerless. Maybe there are supernatural powers that help Tanzanian activists, or should I say the heavens are plotting to help Tanzanian activists as long as they have good will. I submit myself to the greatness of God who saved Tundu Lissu from the valley of the shadow of death after the thirty-eight-shot attack in which sixteen hit several parts of his body, and at the same time, I reflect on the wonders of God who allowed Magufuli to leave the world suddenly. The brutal and torture I went through with many CHADEMA members, the brutal treatment aimed out to activists who opposed Magufuli government was not enough to silence the people. In the human mind, it would be expected now that the rulers would enjoy a state of supremacy after carrying out many horrific events, but this is the first time the noise has increased. Aluta Continua.

It is time for the rulers of Tanzania to learn that, "In order for development to be achieved there must be positive and negative' thoughts. These cannot be killed by force, but by working for them in a civilized manner while defending human rights. If power were to weaken, the argument Magufuli's five years of ruling by an iron hand would have been more than enough. But it was not. Well! There is no enough time to use force to weaken the argument."

But our country is very fortunate. How fortunate that the incidents of people being abducted, tortured and killed were countered by arguments and not by retaliation. As a member and leader of CHADEMA, I know my party has a large number of members and an army of supporters who, if convinced could retaliate by abducting, torturing, and losing CCM members— in the same way that CCM government did against CHADEMA youths. But we can never do that. If CHADEMA decided to take revenge in the same way, it means that, not only would our country go into worse times, but also the party would lose the legitimacy to condemn such evils. If CHADEMA opposes the atrocities committed against us, then we should not harm others. Personally, I have been arrested by soldiers I know, I ended up in severe torture, and there are others who were abducted by soldiers I know, and was later tortured, CCM government officials who were involved in the torture against CHADEMA are known, those who preached hatred are known. In short, the CCM agents of torture for dissidents who were called anonymous are known. If CHADEMA were a party of the wicked, it would retaliate accordingly. But our struggle is argumentative. Our strength is in the argument.

I will continue the struggle with arguments, this time living with the dictatorial remains of Magufuli. I will never touch a person's skin for the sake of hurting him, although it is known that the ignorant hurt their hearts and then want to heal themselves by hurting other people. Those are the people who use force, who have failed and continue to fail. The heavens have rejected them with clear evidence.

Aluta Continua.

IMPORTANT REFERENCES

1. Proceedings of case number No. 136 of 2020

2. Copy of case judgment No. 136 of 2020

3. News; Star TV Facebook page

4. News; Global TV You Tube channel, 29 May 2019

5. News; BBC Kiswahili website, 10 May 2019

6. News; *The Citizen Magazine,* July 28, 2021

7. News; DW Website, 9 May 2019

8. News: *Bagamoyo First* blog

9. News; Radio Ushindi FM—Mbeya

10. News; Jamiiforums blog, 23 Nov. 2021

11. News; Mwanahalisionline blog, 28 June 2021

PHOTOS ON EVENTS

"On 10th May 2019, continuing treatment at Mbeya Referral Hospital. It is after intense persecution by the special squad of the police force tasked to silent Magufuli's criticizers. This was on 13 May 2020, when I was arraigned in the court for drug trafficking. Sitting in front at my right is the Mbeya RCO Regional Criminal Investigation Officer, Katimbo with his aides. No relatives knew that day I would be brought to court on 28 June 2021, in the courtroom awaiting sentencing."